REJOICE NOW

Also by Collective Healing Anonymous

Collective Healing Anonymous Basics

Life Beyond Death

www.discoverCHA.org

Collective Healing Anonymous
in collaboration with Peace President

REJOICE NOW

*365 Days of Loving
Inspiration and Reflection*

C
H A Collective Healing Anonymous
Planet Earth

Collective Healing Anonymous
Planet Earth

© 2025 Collective Healing Anonymous

ISBN 978-0-9862276-5-3

Contents

Appendices

The CHA Dedication

Collective Healing Anonymous (CHA) is a loving invitation and compassionate opportunity to be deeply honest with ourselves through a revolutionary non-religious, yet highly spiritual, Twelve Step Process toward healing, feeling, and awakening. As we begin realizing our primal innocence and truth of ourselves through this journey of self-love, forgiveness, and acceptance, we rediscover our natural wholeness and worthiness that never left. By sincerely acknowledging and healing whatever obsessions, compulsions, addictions, and identity challenges holding us back from living a life of everlasting inner freedom and joyful peacefulness, we reclaim autonomy of our body and mind. As willing and grateful participants of CHA and Life, we dedicate ourselves to genuine inner transformation, peaceful coexistence, and Self-Realization—Enlightenment.

Introduction

This book is an invitation into the sacred rhythm of daily reflection, healing, and awakening. Rooted in the spirit of Collective Healing Anonymous, these pages offer gentle guidance, honest inquiry, and moments of presence to support your journey toward greater inner freedom and clarity. Each day's reflection is a doorway—a chance to pause, breathe, and return to what truly matters.

Rather than offering rigid beliefs or doctrines, this daily reader encourages direct experience. It honors the intelligence already within you, and the living presence that moves through all things. These words are not meant to be followed, but felt—to stir something real in your heart, your body, and your being.

Whether you are walking through grief or gratitude, confusion or clarity, may this book meet you where you are and remind you: you are not alone, you are already whole, and awakening is a natural unfolding. One day, one breath, one truth at a time.

Let these pages be your loving and gentle practice of recognizing, embracing, and feeling the wholeness, grace, and loving awareness that you already are, always.

JANUARY 1

Rejoice Now

Life is not something to endure—it is something to rejoice in. Right now, in this very moment, you are alive. Your heart beats, your breath flows, and your awareness illuminates the miracle of mind, and simply being here. Rejoicing is not about waiting for the "perfect" moment—it is recognizing that now is always the time to celebrate life.

Even in the midst of uncertainty, there is always something to rejoice in. The warmth of the sun on your skin, the rhythm of your breath, the ability to feel, to think, to love. To be human is to experience the vastness of existence, to witness the unfolding of life with wonder. Today, take a moment to rejoice. Not because of something external, but simply because you are here. You are alive!

I rejoice in the gift of being alive, knowing that each moment is an opportunity to celebrate life.

JANUARY 2

Be Gentle with Yourself

In a world that often demands toughness and speed, gentleness can feel like a forgotten possibility. But gentleness is not weakness—it's a profound strength. It takes courage to soften your inner dialogue, to approach yourself and others with kindness instead of judgment.

Today, practice gentleness with yourself. Notice any harsh self-talk or moments where you rush your body or mind. Instead, slow down. Speak to yourself as you would to a dear friend. As the innocent and tender life that you are. Treat your actions as though they are sacred and deliberate, and guided by unconditional love.

I honor myself and others with the gift of gentleness.

JANUARY 3

Handling Conflict with Others

Conflict with others often feels like a storm, but much of the turbulence comes from within. We project our fears, assumptions, and insecurities onto the situation, magnifying its intensity. The first step to handling conflict is to pause, breathe, and look inward.

Ask yourself: What am I feeling right now? What story am I telling myself about this situation? Often, what seems like external conflict is an opportunity to reflect on unresolved emotions or unmet needs within ourselves. Approach the situation with curiosity, not defensiveness, and allow compassion to guide your response.

I meet conflict with curiosity, awareness, and a desire to understand.

JANUARY 4

Authenticity

Authenticity is the courage to live in alignment with your true self, even when the world pressures you to conform. It means letting go of the masks you wear to gain approval or avoid judgment and allowing your thoughts, feelings, and actions to reflect who you really are.

Today, reflect on areas of your life where you feel the most yourself. How can you bring that same energy to spaces where you feel guarded or hesitant? Remember, authenticity isn't about being perfect—it's about being real, with all your unique strengths and seeming imperfections.

I embrace my true-self with courage and trust.

JANUARY 5

The Power of Attention

Where your attention goes, your energy flows. When you allow your attention to drift aimlessly or fixate on negativity, you give your power away to the egoic-mind. But when you consciously choose to direct your attention—toward gratitude, connection, or the present moment—you reclaim your ability to shape your inner experience.

Today, practice observing where your attention tends to settle. Is it on worries or self-judgment? Pause, take a breath, and gently guide it toward something uplifting—a kind thought, a peaceful moment, or the beauty around you.

I choose to focus on what nourishes all aspects of my being.

JANUARY 6

Asking for Help

Asking for help is not a sign of weakness but an act of courage and trust. It requires us to set aside pride, fear, or the belief that we must face life's challenges alone. Equally important is allowing ourselves to receive help without conditions—without guilt, shame, or the need to "earn" it. Help is a gift, and accepting it with an open heart creates connection and healing.

Today, reflect on where you might need support. Can you ask for help without judgment or hesitation? And if help comes your way, practice receiving it with grace and gratitude, knowing that you are worthy of care and kindness.

I open myself to ask for and receive help with trust and gratitude.

Saying Yes to Life

Saying yes to life means opening your heart to the full range of experiences it offers—the joys, the challenges, and everything in between. It's an act of trust, a willingness to embrace each moment as it comes, without resistance or fear. When we say yes, we stop fighting against life and begin to flow with it, discovering opportunities for growth and connection we might have otherwise missed.

Today, practice saying yes to what life presents. Notice where you might habitually resist or close off, and instead, lean into curiosity and acceptance. By saying yes, you create space for life to unfold in ways that serve your highest good.

I shout "YES!" from the mountain tops and embrace life with openness, trust, and gratitude.

Mercy

Mercy is the act of offering compassion and forgiveness, even when it feels undeserved. It is a gift we give to others and to ourselves, softening the harsh edges of judgment and allowing healing to take root. Mercy doesn't excuse harm but acknowledges our shared humanity—the mistakes, struggles, and imperfections we all carry.

Today, reflect on where you might extend mercy in your life. Is there a situation, a person, or even a place in the body that would benefit from releasing the weight of judgment and hardness? Mercy is not weakness; it is the strength to live and lead with compassion and understanding.

I choose mercy as a pathway to healing and connection.

Life is a Celebration

Every moment of life holds something worth celebrating. It might be the simple beauty of sunlight streaming through a window, the warmth of connection with a friend, or the quiet joy of taking a deep, steady breath. When we choose to see life as a celebration, even small moments become sacred, and we awaken to the abundance around us.

Today, look for reasons to celebrate. Find joy in the little things—an unexpected smile, a kind word, or the rhythm of your own heartbeat. Life is a gift, and each moment is an opportunity to honor it with gratitude and wonder.

I celebrate the beauty and joy in life's simple moments.

Fire

Fire is the element of transformation, passion, and vitality. It symbolizes the inner flame that fuels our drive for growth and change, burning away what no longer serves us to make room for new beginnings. Like a fire's flickering warmth, it can comfort and inspire, yet it also demands respect for its power to reshape and renew.

Today, connect with your inner fire. What in your life is ready to be transformed? Allow this sacred element to ignite your passion, burn away stagnation, and illuminate your path forward. Fire reminds us that within destruction lies the promise of renewal.

I honor the fire within as a force for growth and transformation.

<hr>

JANUARY 11

Reclaiming Autonomy

Reclaiming autonomy begins with a humble acknowledgment of the ways we have leaned on coping mechanisms to navigate life's challenges. Whether it's a dependency on behaviors, substances, or thought patterns, these mechanisms were temporary solutions, not lasting answers. By recognizing their impact, we take the first step toward reclaiming the power within us to shape our minds, choices, and lives with conscious intention.

Today, reflect on where you might be giving away your autonomy. Are there habits or patterns holding you back? Gently remind yourself that you hold the power to change, and embrace this step forward with courage and self-compassion.

I honor my inner strength and reclaim the freedom of my mind.

<hr>

JANUARY 12

Equanimity

Equanimity is the calm within the storm, the inner balance that allows us to face life's highs and lows with grace and steadiness. It does not mean indifference; rather, it is the wisdom to remain centered, knowing that all experiences—joyful and difficult—are temporary. Equanimity invites us to meet life with an open heart, free from reactivity or attachment.

Today, when challenges arise, take a moment to pause and breathe. Remind yourself that this moment, too, is already passing; for all experiencing is fleeting, impermanent, constantly changing. Cultivate the strength to remain calm and compassionate, trusting in your ability to navigate life with peace and clarity.

I remain balanced and open,
grounded in the wisdom and inner security of equanimity.

JANUARY 13

The Importance of Humor

Humor is a powerful tool for healing and connection, offering lightness to moments that might otherwise feel heavy. True humor is not rooted in sarcasm or passive aggression but in joy, playfulness, and a shared understanding of our human experience. It softens the edges of life's challenges and reminds us not to take ourselves too seriously.

Today, look for opportunities to embrace humor in its purest form. Laugh at the small absurdities of life, share a moment of joy with someone, or allow yourself to play. Genuine humor uplifts and unites, creating space for love and resilience to grow.

I invite joy and lightness into my life through the gift of humor.

JANUARY 14

Relaxing into the Hard Times

The seeming hard times often feel like storms we must fight against, but resistance only deepens the struggle. Almost always, we discover "Things were not as bad as my mind made them out to be." When we allow ourselves to relax into what feels unbearable or difficult, we create space for wisdom and tenderness to emerge. Surrendering doesn't mean giving up—it means softening our grip, letting go of the need to control, and trusting that even the hardest moments can carry invaluable wisdom and conscious clarity.

Today, notice areas where you may be resisting life. Take a deep breath and allow yourself to release tension, even if just for a moment. Trust that by surrendering, you open the door to deeper understanding.

I surrender to life's challenges with trust, knowing they hold wisdom for my journey.

JANUARY 15

The Power of Self-Inquiry

Self-inquiry is a profound practice that invites us to question the beliefs and assumptions we hold about ourselves and the world. By asking questions like, "Who am I beneath my thoughts?" or "Is this belief truly serving me?" we begin to uncover the deeper truths of our nature. This process helps us release outdated patterns and illusions, allowing us to align more fully with authenticity and inner peace.

Today, take a few moments to turn inward. When a strong emotion or belief arises, ask yourself, "What is beneath this? What truth am I ready to see?" Through self-inquiry, you awaken to the power and clarity already within you. When we willingly and ever so gently open our hearts and minds to attending to our inner world through self-inquiry, we naturally begin healing in ways beyond measure.

I explore my inner world with gentle curiosity,
seeking the non mental truth of who I am.

Welcoming the Flow of Experience

Welcoming is an act of opening your heart to the full flow of life—the joys, the challenges, and everything in between. It means saying "yes" to all aspects of your experience, embracing each moment as an opportunity for healing, feeling, and awakening. When we resist life, we create tension, but in welcoming, we discover a natural harmony that allows us to move with life's currents instead of against them.

Today, practice welcoming what arises, whether it feels pleasant or uncomfortable. Greet each experience with curiosity and compassion, trusting that every moment holds the potential for growth and transformation.

I welcome all aspects of my experience, trusting in life's unfolding flow.

Gratitude

Gratitude is a powerfully loving force that transforms the way we experience life. When we focus on what we have rather than what we lack, we shift our perspective from scarcity to abundance. Gratitude doesn't ignore challenges but reminds us of the beauty and blessings that coexist alongside them. It opens our hearts to the richness of life, deepens our connections, and brings a sense of peace.

Today, take a moment to reflect on three things you are grateful for. They can be as simple as the breath you're taking now, the warmth of sunlight, or the presence of someone you love. Allow gratitude to fill you and remind you of the countless gifts life offers.

I embrace gratitude as a source of joy, peace, and connection.

Opening to Possibility

When we cling too tightly to familiar beliefs or outcomes, we limit ourselves to what we already know. Opening to possibility means releasing the need to control and allowing space for life to surprise us. It invites creativity, opportunities, and solutions we may not have imagined. Possibility exists in every moment, waiting for us to say yes to new paths and perspectives.

Today, notice where you might be holding onto rigid expectations. What would happen if you let go of those limitations? Allow yourself to open to the unknown and trust that life has possibilities far greater than you can foresee.

I release control and open my heart to infinite possibilities.

Cultivating

Within each of us lies the potential for sacred qualities such as compassion, kindness, patience, and softness to flourish. These qualities may feel distant at times, especially during hardship, but like seeds, they grow when we nurture them with intention and practice. Cultivating them requires gentle persistence—choosing to act from the heart even when it feels difficult; even when the mind wants to do or say something unkind. Each time we choose kindness over anger or compassion over judgment, we strengthen these inner virtues.

Today, reflect on which sacred quality you would like to cultivate. How can you practice embodying that quality in small ways throughout your day? Remember, growth is a process, and each moment of practice nourishes your spirit.

I cultivate sacred qualities within me,
allowing them to guide my thoughts, words, and actions.

JANUARY 20

Spontaneous

Life is inherently spontaneous—a continuous, ever-changing flow that unfolds moment by moment. Beneath the mind's need to plan, control, and predict, there is a deeper essence of life that moves freely and intuitively. When we align with this presence within us, we become part of the natural rhythm of life. We act not from force or calculation but from a place of flow, allowing our thoughts, feelings, and actions to arise naturally.

Today, practice letting go of control and allow yourself to move with life's spontaneity. Notice moments where your body and mind already know how to respond without overthinking—trust in that inner presence guiding you.

I live in harmony with the spontaneous flow of life, trusting the presence
within me.

JANUARY 21

Redemption

Redemption is the process of reclaiming the truth of who we are beneath our mistakes, pain, and past choices. It is not about erasing what has happened but about transforming it—finding meaning, growth, and healing in the experiences that shaped us. True redemption begins with self-forgiveness, recognizing that we are not defined by our past but by how we choose to move forward.

Today, reflect on any burdens you carry from past actions or regrets. Can you offer yourself compassion and see the lessons they've brought you? Redemption invites you to rise anew, empowered by the wisdom gained from every experience.

I release the past and embrace the redemptive power of healing and growth.

JANUARY 22

Company

True company is not just about being surrounded by others but about sharing moments of genuine connection. When we are truly present with someone—without judgment or distraction—we create a space for both giving and receiving support. When we genuinely listen to what others are saying without trying to think of how to respond, or attempting to predict what they are going to say, is when we strengthen our connection with our deepest being. Likewise, we can learn to offer company to ourselves by becoming present with our inner world, honoring our thoughts and feelings with compassion. When we listen to what our inner world is saying, what feelings are saying, feelings of loneliness subside.

Today, practice being fully present with those around you and with your inner world. Offer your attention and presence as a gift, free from distraction. Notice how moments of connection deepen when you meet experience with openness and care—genuinely listening.

I cultivate meaningful presence,
offering and receiving the gift of true company.

Respect

Respect begins with recognizing the innate value in yourself and others. It calls for honoring each person's unique journey, even when it differs from your own. When we practice respect, we listen without interruption, seek understanding over judgment, and hold space for both ourselves and others to be authentic.

Today, reflect on how you can bring more respect to your interactions. Do you offer yourself the same kindness and consideration that you offer others? Respect thrives when it flows in both directions—toward others and within.

I honor the inherent dignity in myself and others through respect.

Balance

Balance is not a rigid state but a dynamic process, like the ebb and flow of the tides. It invites us to remain centered as we navigate the demands of life, ensuring we tend to our physical, emotional, and spiritual needs. When we ignore balance, we feel drained and scattered, but when we nurture it, life flows with greater ease and harmony.

Today, take a moment to reflect on the areas of your life where balance may be missing. Is there space to rest, reflect, or reconnect with what matters most? Small adjustments can restore your sense of wholeness.

I create balance by honoring my needs and staying
present with life's flow.

Praise

Praise is a way of celebrating life's goodness, whether through recognizing the strengths of others or acknowledging your own efforts. Offering praise from a sincere heart uplifts those around us and strengthens bonds of trust and connection. Equally important is learning to give yourself praise—not as self-flattery, but as a form of kindness that encourages growth.

Today, offer praise where it is due. Recognize someone's effort, resilience, or kindness, and reflect on your own strengths. Praise is a gift that brings joy and affirmation to both the giver and receiver.

I celebrate the goodness within myself and others with heartfelt praise.

Oh Well…?

There are moments when life doesn't go as planned, and frustration or disappointment threatens to take over. In those moments, a simple shift in perspective can make all the difference. Saying "Oh well" isn't about indifference—it's about learning to let go, surrendering to what is beyond your control, and allowing peace to replace resistance. With an attitude of loving surrender and absolute acceptance, see how it feels to say, "Oh well…?"

Today, when things don't appear to go your way, pause and take a deep breath. Ask yourself, "Is this worth my peace? Is what's happening right here now allowed to be as it is?" Letting go may reveal opportunities and lessons hidden in the unexpected.

I release resistance and trust in life's greater flow.

JANUARY 27

Paradox

Life is full of paradoxes—apparent contradictions that hold deeper truths. We find strength through vulnerability, freedom through earnest focus, and peace by embracing both joy and sorrow. Accepting life's paradoxes allows us to live more fully, without the need for rigid answers or certainty.

Today, reflect on a paradox that shows up in your life. What lesson does it offer you? By holding space for these seeming contradictions, you open yourself to a deeper understanding of life's complexity and beauty; and most of all, it's mystery.

I embrace the paradoxes of life, trusting the mysterious wisdom they reveal.

JANUARY 28

I AM

Who are you beyond your roles, thoughts, and emotions? The statement "I AM" invites you to explore your true nature, beyond the labels and identities you have acquired. In this inquiry, you may discover that your essence is not tied to external definitions but is an expansive, ever-present awareness. The 'I AM' sense of existence is always here prior to claiming I am this or that. Humbly allow your attention to notice your 'I AM-ness.'

Today, take a few moments to sit in stillness and ask yourself, "Who am I, really?" Don't seek an answer—simply rest in the experience of being and allow your awareness to unfold.

I am infinite presence, free from limitation and definition. I AM.

Perceiving

Long before the mind assigns meaning, before thoughts create labels, perceiving is already happening. The power of perceiving is always on—it is the silent awareness through which all experience flows. A tree is seen before it is named, a sound is heard before it is judged, a sensation is felt before it is analyzed.

When we rest in pure perceiving—without rushing to categorize, define, or interpret—we experience life directly, as it is. This is the space of clarity, free from the distortions of mental narratives. The world becomes more vivid, more alive, when we simply perceive without immediately believing every thought that arises.

Today, practice noticing perceiving before the mind interferes. See before you name, listen before you interpret, feel before you explain. Experience the world as it is, not as the mind tells you it should be.

I rest in the power of pure perceiving, allowing experience to arise without the need to define or control it.

Strength

True strength is not about force or control but about resilience and inner stability. It is the ability to face life's challenges with compassionate courage, trust, and grace. Strength emerges not from denying vulnerability but from embracing it, knowing that your inner core remains unshaken by temporary storms.

Today, connect with your inner strength. Recall a time when

you overcame a challenge and grew through the experience. Trust that this strength is always within you, ready to guide you through whatever comes next.

I draw on the deep well of strength within
me to face life with courage and grace.

JANUARY 31

Flowing

Flowing with life means letting go of resistance and moving with the natural rhythms of experience. It is about trusting that life is unfolding as it should, even when you cannot see the full picture. When you release the need to control, you allow yourself to dance with life's ever-changing current.

Today, practice flowing by embracing flexibility. When plans change or obstacles arise, pause and breathe. Allow life to carry you forward instead of pushing against it; freely flowing into the unknown.

I move with life's flow, trusting in its natural unfolding.

FEBRUARY 1

Equality

Equality acknowledges the inherent worth and dignity in all beings. When we honor equality, we dissolve the barriers of superiority and inferiority, recognizing that beneath surface differences, we are all deeply connected. This awareness invites us to treat everyone—including ourselves—with fairness, compassion, and respect.

Today, reflect on how you can embody equality. Are there places where you compare yourself to others or judge based on appearances? Practice honoring the shared humanity in all by seeing everyone and everything as your very SELF.

I honor the deep equality and connection among all beings.
We are ALL one.

FEBRUARY 2

Universal Consciousness

Universal Consciousness is the infinitely loving awareness that witnesses all of life's experiences. It is the space within which thoughts, emotions, and sensations arise and dissolve. It is the ever-present reality from which the body and mind appear in consciousness. By deepening our connection to this inner awareness, we begin to see that we are more than our temporary experiences—that we are not the body and not even the mind. We are the very divine presence—the underlying loving awareness that holds all experiencing.

Today, turn your attention inward. Notice the loving awareness that observes your thoughts and feelings—the body and the mind.

This Universal Consciousness is always present, the source of everything, offering peace, serenity and clarity, always herenow.

I rest in the loving presence of pure universal consciousness that I AM, witnessing life with openness and peace.

Experiencing

Experiencing life fully means allowing yourself to feel and be present with all that arises. Rather than rejecting difficult emotions or clinging to pleasurable ones, open your heart to the full spectrum of life. In this openness, you discover that every experience, no matter how fleeting, has something to teach and transform you.

Today, practice being fully present with your experiences. Notice the sensations, thoughts, and emotions as they arise, without judgment or resistance. Notice how they are fleeting, impermanent, never last; and allow yourself to be fully alive in this moment. Allowing everything to be as it is.

I embrace the richness of life by being fully present with all aspects of experiencing that never lasts.

Transformation

Transformation is not a single moment but an ongoing journey of becoming consciously clear as mature and infinitely loving human beings. Life constantly invites us to grow, shed old patterns, and embrace new ways of being in love with life. Often, the most profound transformations occur quietly—through moments of awareness, small shifts in perspective, and acts of courage that open doors to change.

Today, reflect on how you've transformed over the past year. What old habits or beliefs have you outgrown? What layers have you allowed to be shed? Trust that every experience, even the difficult ones, serves the unfolding of your highest loving potential.

I embrace transformation as a natural and continuous part of life.

Sensing

Our senses are gateways to presence. By tuning into the sensations of life—the warmth of sunlight, the rhythm of breath, leaves rustling in the wind, the sounds of the world—we awaken to the richness of the moment. Sensing deeply connects us to both our inner and outer worlds, grounding us in the herenow.

Today, take time to pause and engage your senses fully. Notice the details of your surroundings and how your body feels in the present moment. Smell the air. Taste the fragrances of life. Allow sensing to guide you into deeper presence.

I fully engage my senses, awakening to the beauty of the present moment

FEBRUARY 6

Allowing

Allowing means softening into life as it is, without forcing or resisting. It is an act of trust, accepting that each moment holds both possibility and grace; regardless of what the mind mentally attaches to what is happening. When we allow rather than control, we create space for healing, growth, and new possibilities to emerge naturally.

Today, notice where you may be holding onto resistance, temporarily stuck in the mind that wants 'right-here-now' to be other than what it is. With a kind and gentle heart, take a breath and practice allowing—letting things be as they are. Trust that by loosening your mental grip on the experience you are having, life can unfold with greater ease and wisdom.

I allow life to flow through me, trusting in the unfolding of each moment. I am tender.

FEBRUARY 7

Secure-ness

True security comes not from external circumstances, from not getting what the mind believes it wants, but from within. It arises when we trust in our ability to navigate life's uncertainties with grace and compassionate understanding. By connecting to the steady presence inside us, the ever-present loving awareness that we are, we find a sense of secure-ness that no outside condition can take away. We no longer rely on people, places, things, or specific situations or feelings to provide us with the secure sense of self we have been seeking for most of our lives.

Today, reflect on where you seek security. Is it tied to something outside of yourself? Gently return your focus inward, grounding yourself in the inner strength and stability that is always present; knowing that perfect love casts out all fear.

I rest in the secure-ness of my inner presence as love itself.

Discovery

Discovery is an ever-present possibility, waiting in the ordinary moments of life. When we remain curious and open, even the smallest experiences can reveal new insights and deeper truths. Discovery isn't limited to the world outside—most importantly, it involves exploring the vast inner world of our thoughts, emotions, and intuition.

Today, approach your day with curiosity. What can you discover about yourself, others, or your environment that you've never noticed before? Allow discovery to expand your awareness and appreciation of life.

I open myself to the endless discoveries within and around me.

Thankfulness

Thankfulness is a practice of honoring the abundance already present in your life. When we cultivate thankfulness, we shift our focus from what is missing to what is here, inviting more joy and contentment into our experience. It helps us see the beauty in the smallest things—a smile, a shared moment, or the steady support of our breath.

Today, take a few moments to express thankfulness. Reflect on what has nourished you and those who have touched your life with kindness. Let gratitude guide your thoughts and actions throughout the day.

I live in a state of thankfulness, honoring the gifts of life.
I am LIFE itself!

Within

The most profound truths are found within. While the outer world with its practical purpose may distract and demand your attention, there is a quiet loving presence inside you that holds infinite peace and everlasting clarity and serenity. By turning inward, you reconnect with your essence—the stillness that is untouched by the noise of life. The timeless loving awareness that you are.

Today, take time to sit in silence and listen to the presence within. Let it guide you and remind you that everything you seek already resides inside you, lovingly.

I trust the wisdom and stillness within me.
I am already secure, peaceful, fulfilled.

Not Knowing

We often seek certainty, but life is a dance with the unknown. Embracing 'not knowing' is an act of humility and trust, allowing us to remain open to new possibilities and insights; and unconditional love. When we let go of the need to have all the answers, we create space for growth and discovery as the energy of arrogance is transmuted into humility.

Today, reflect on an area of your life where you feel uncertain. Can you soften into that space, allowing 'not knowing' to bring clarity in its own time? Trust that wisdom arises when we release the need to control.

I embrace not knowing,
trusting life to reveal what I need in its perfect time.

Acceptance

Acceptance is the foundation of peace. It does not mean resigning yourself to a harmful situation or indignant circumstances but rather seeing things clearly as they are, without resistance. Through loving acceptance, we create the conditions for healing and transformation, as we release the struggle against reality and meet life and experience with openness and love.

Today, with a loving heart, practice accepting something you have been resisting. Perhaps it is a situation or a feeling. Notice how acceptance brings a sense of calm and clarity, allowing you to respond with greater wisdom and compassion beyond a reactive fearful mind.

I accept life and what I am feeling as it is, trusting in the power of presence and peace. I AM Here.

What isn't a Miracle?

Life itself is a miracle. Every breath, every heartbeat, every blade of grass growing in the sunlight is part of a vast, interconnected dance. When we open our eyes to the wonder of life's unfolding, we see that miracles are not rare—they are everywhere, waiting to be noticed. In fact, everything is a miracle!

Today, ask yourself: What isn't a miracle? Look for the extraordinary in the ordinary and allow a sense of awe to fill your heart.

I open my heart to the miraculous beauty in all things.

Purity

Purity is not about perfection but about aligning with the essence of who you truly are. It is a state of being unclouded by fear, judgment, or pretense. When we release the layers of conditioning and return to our authentic nature, when we no longer believe what the mind is saying, we rediscover the purity of presence, compassion, and truth within us.

Today, reflect on how you can reconnect with your inner purity. Notice moments when you are fully present and free of judgment. Notice what it feels like to not believe thoughts. What happens? Allow yourself to experience life with a fresh, open heart and mind free of false assumptions and beliefs.

I accept the purity of my authentic being; for it has never left.

Vibrations

Everything in the universe is energy, vibrating in unique frequencies. Our thoughts, emotions, and intentions carry vibrations that influence the world around us and within us. When we cultivate higher vibrations—such as love, gratitude, generosity, and kindness—we elevate our experiences and attract harmony and peace into our lives.

Today, tune into the vibrations you are carrying. Are they aligned with the life you want to create? Gently shift your inner state by focusing on uplifting thoughts, feelings, and actions.

I attune myself to the vibrations of love, peace, and joy.

Receiving

True receiving is an act of openness, trust, and unconditional love. Many of us feel more comfortable giving than receiving, often placing conditions on the care we accept. Yet life flows through both giving and receiving, unconditionally. When we allow ourselves to receive fully with grace and gratitude—beyond the reaction to return the kind act—we honor the abundance of life.

Today, practice receiving unconditionally without resistance. Whether it's a compliment, a kind gesture, or simply the gift of breath, open your heart and accept it fully.

I welcome and receive the gifts of life with openness and gratitude.

Air

Air is life's gentle presence, one of the five essential elements of all creation that makes life possible—the practical power of prana we can feel, the vital energy moving through and around us at every moment. It sustains us, yet we often take it for granted. Air reminds us of the importance of stillness, balance, and the unseen forces that sustain life. By tuning into the element of air, we become more present, aware of the miracle of each breath—the communion with nature all around us.

Today, take moments to connect with your breath. Notice how each inhale and exhale grounds and centers you. Let air remind you of the sacred interdependent and interconnected flow of life.

I honor the life-giving presence of air in every breath;
the life force energy flowing through me.

Serenity

Serenity is the calm that arises when we release resistance and trust the flow of life. It does not depend on external circumstances but on our inner willingness to accept things as they are. When we cultivate serenity by trusting our unshakable loving presence, we find ourselves more easily able to face life's challenges with grace and emotional resilience.

Today, take a moment to rest in stillness. Breathe deeply and allow serenity to fill your heart and mind, for it is always abundantly here, within, when we allow our attention to look. Let go of any tension or worries and trust in the peace that already resides within you.

I cultivate serenity by releasing resistance and embracing inner peace.

Tenderness

Like a Mother who loves you unconditionally, no matter what, tenderness is a gentle, nurturing energy that invites connection and healing. It requires vulnerability and openness, allowing us to meet ourselves and others with kindness and care; regardless of what the mind is saying. By embracing tenderness as our inner Mother, we soften the edges of pain and create space for love to flow freely.

Today, approach yourself and others with tenderness. Notice how small acts of kindness and gentleness can transform your experience. Tenderness is not weakness—it is the humble strength that holds infinite space for infinite compassion.

I offer tenderness to myself and others,
nurturing healing and connection.

Smiles

A smile is a simple yet profound gesture that carries warmth and kindness. It can uplift both the giver and the receiver, bridging connections without words. Even a smile directed inward—toward yourself—can shift your emotional state, inviting joy and peace into your day.

Today, practice smiling consciously. Smile at yourself, at strangers, and at loved ones. Notice how this simple act changes the energy around you and within you.

I share the warmth and light of a smile, spreading kindness and joy.

Nurturing

Nurturing is the act of providing care and attention to what is asking for loving attention, growth, and healing. This applies not only to others but, most importantly, to yourself. When you nurture your inner world—your dreams, emotions, and well-being— you create a foundation for flourishing and transformation that affects everything. Just as a plant thrives when given water, sunlight, and care, you, too, require nourishment—emotionally, mentally, and spiritually. Nurturing is not indulgence; it is an essential act of self-honoring that allows you to show up more fully in life.

Today, ask yourself: What in my life is asking for nurturing attention right now? Offer yourself the care and presence needed for compassionate growth and expansion.

I nurture myself and others with love and kind intention.

Adoration

Adoration is a deep reverence and appreciation for the beauty and wonder of life. And not necessarily physical beauty, but the intangible and invisible beauty of all creation. It arises when we allow ourselves to fully experience awe—whether toward nature, a person, or the divine essence within us all. Through adoration, we reconnect with the sacredness of existence.

Today, find a moment to adore something or someone in your life. Let yourself be filled with appreciation and wonder. Notice how this deepens your sense of connection, presence, and unconditional love for all beings.

I open my heart to adoration, honoring the sacred beauty in everything.

Doing – Taking Action

There are times for reflection and times for apparent conscious action. Taking conscious action moves us forward on our journey and brings dreams and intentions into reality. However, meaningful action arises not from pressure or fear, but from alignment with purpose and intuition.

Today, reflect on one action you can take to support your goals or well-being. Even small steps have the power to create momentum. Trust your intuition prior to mind's conflicted negotiations to guide you toward the right action for this moment.

I take inspired action, trusting in the power of aligned doing;
being in integrity with all that is.

Fairness

Fairness is rooted in justice and equality, recognizing the inherent worth of all beings. Not the ideas of justice and concepts of equality that are products of opinion and bias, but true unconditional fairness. It invites us to consider others' needs and perspectives with an open mind and heart beyond our personal conditioning and judgments. True fairness does not favor one over another but seeks balance, ensuring that compassion and integrity guide our actions.

Today, reflect on how you can bring fairness into your interactions. Are there places where you can offer compassionate understanding or unconditional equality? Let fairness lead your choices and create harmony in your relationships. Listening more, talking less.

I practice fairness by honoring the needs and worth of all.

Trust

Trust is the foundation of all meaningful relationships, including the one you have with your experiencing. It grows through consistency, honesty, and openness. When we trust, we release fear and control, allowing life to unfold as it is meant to. We trust that our feelings, no matter how intense, cannot harm us. Trusting yourself means believing in your ability to handle whatever comes your way.

Today, notice where trust may be missing in your life. Can you take one step to rebuild or deepen it? Trust begins with small acts of faith and grows with each moment of truthfulness and presence.

I trust myself, others, and life's unfolding path.

Discipline (Not Punishment)

As a Kung-fu Master relentlessly refines their martial arts discipline, so is our plight to become the master of the mind's mental Discipline. Discipline, in this sense, is an act of love, not punishment—but conscious effort to reclaim autonomy of our minds through the mental discipline of focusing our kind and loving attention how we see fit. It is the practice of committing to what nourishes and strengthens you. Discipline (or diligent one-pointed focus) builds resilience and clarity, helping the mind stay aligned with your values and goals. Unlike punishment, which comes from judgment and fear, discipline is earnestly focusing attention, rooted in self-respect and loving kindness.

Today, reflect on how remaining focused can support your well-being. What small, intentional step can you take to stay in alignment with your highest calling? Approach mental discipline with kindness and encouragement. Not beating yourself up but merely concentrating on the task at hand. That is the loving essence of mental discipline, not punishment.

I honor myself through loving, supportive concentration of attention.

Movement

Movement is life in action. Whether through physical activity, creative expression, or emotional growth, movement keeps us connected to the dynamic flow of existence. It releases stagnation and invites energy and renewal. When we embrace movement with awareness, we create space for transformation, joy, and playfulness.

Today, move with intention. Whether it's a walk, a dance, or simply stretching your body, feel how movement connects you to life's pulse. Let it bring vitality and presence to your day. Get up, open the door, and walk outside without any destination in mind; merely watching where your feet carry you.

I flow with life's energy through mindful, joyful movement.

FEBRUARY 28

Grace

Grace is the quiet strength that carries us through life's challenges with dignity and ease. It is the ability to move gently, forgive easily, and trust deeply. Grace allows us to soften our defenses and approach both ourselves and others with compassion and softness; even in difficult moments where we feel rigid and defensive.

Today, invite grace into your life. Notice where you might be holding tension or judgment, and gently let it go. All you have to do is say, "Grace. Grace. Grace." And watch and feel. Trust in the flow of life and allow grace to guide your thoughts and actions.

I move through life with grace, trusting in its gentle power.

FEBRUARY 29

Stability

Stability is not about rigid control but about finding inner grounding amid life's constant changes. It comes from cultivating practices, beliefs, and relationships that support your well-being. When you are stable within yourself, external turbulence has less power to shake your peace.

Today, reflect on what brings you a sense of stability. How can you strengthen your foundation—physically, emotionally, or spiritually? Perhaps embracing Sacred Processes like Yoga, Nature Immersion, or Meditation, rather than watching more television, eating more unhealthy foods, or being lost in social media, can be a loving possibility—new life affirming habits consciously focused on genuine well-being. By opening to what your heart already knows would be loving habits to engage in versus those no longer serving you, space and openness to a life of greater peace, resilience, and clarity emerges. And, unconditional love; as love itSELF.

I create stability by opening to Sacred Processes
that serve overall well-being.

MARCH 1

Honesty

Honesty is a pathway to deeper trust and authentic connection. It requires vulnerability and courage to express what is true for you without fear or judgment. Honesty, however, must be guided by kindness—it is not about bluntness, blame, guilt, or shame, but about offering truth in a way that fosters loving growth and compassionate understanding.

Today, practice honesty with yourself. Are there areas where you've been avoiding your truth? Allow honesty and loving tenderness to guide your choices and interactions, creating clarity and alignment.

I honor myself and others by living with honesty and kindness.

MARCH 2

Give Yourself a Break

You don't have to carry the weight of the world every moment. In fact, you don't have to carry the weight of world at all. Life's challenges can be overwhelming, but you deserve moments of rest and kindness. Giving yourself a break doesn't mean you're failing—it means recognizing that you are human and that rest is essential to your well-being.

Today, offer yourself a moment of rest. Let go of any expectations or pressure you've placed on yourself and breathe deeply. Trust that everything you need will unfold in time. And, notice, right here now, that everything is perfectly fine, regardless of what the mind is saying.

I give myself permission to rest and recharge. I am safe already here now.

Compassion

Compassion is the willingness to meet suffering—both in yourself and others—with an open, loving heart. It dissolves the barriers of judgment and invites connection through understanding. Compassion doesn't seek to fix or change OR impose its will through force; but offers presence, empathy, and willingness to unconditionally understand; creating infinite space for healing and authentic expression to unfold.

Today, practice compassion toward yourself. When difficult emotions arise, hold them gently without judgment. Extend the same kindness to others, recognizing the shared humanity in all experiences.

*I cultivate compassion, offering presence and
kindness to myself and others.*

Cosmos

The cosmos is vast and infinite, a reminder of the deep interconnectedness of all life. When we reflect on the stars, galaxies, and the great mystery of existence, we realize that we are part of something far greater than the self-images and self-concepts we have become entranced with. This perspective brings both awe and humility, grounding us in the wonder of life's infinite and timeless unfolding.

Today, take a moment to reflect on your connection to the cosmos. Look at the sky, feel the earth beneath you, and remember that you are a unique expression of this infinite, ever-expanding universe.

*I honor my seeming place in the cosmos,
connected to the infinite wonder of existence.*

MARCH 5

Inclusivity – Absolute Inclusion

Inclusivity honors the truth that every being is already and always valuable and worthy of belonging without the need to earn it. True inclusion embraces not just the diverse ideas of race, gender, and beliefs that divide us from one another, but also the full range of experiences and emotions within ourselves and others. Absolute inclusion recognizes that nothing is separate—every aspect of life is interconnected and essential to the whole.

Today, reflect on how you can practice greater inclusion. Are there parts of yourself or others that you have excluded or judged? Welcome them with compassion, knowing that embracing all of life brings greater unity and healing.

I embrace absolute inclusion,
honoring the worth of all beings and experiences.

MARCH 6

Conscious Action

Conscious action arises from a place of presence and intention. Instead of reacting impulsively or from habit, we pause, reflect, and choose actions aligned with our most loving values. Conscious actions are powerful because they create harmony within ourselves and with the world around us.

Today, practice taking conscious action instead of living reactively on autopilot or the mind's obsessions and compulsions. Before responding to a situation, take a breath and ask yourself, "Is this action aligned with who I really am?" Allow mindfulness to guide your choices.

I take conscious action, aligning my behavior with
kind intention and loving presence.

Restfulness

Restfulness is more than just sleep—it is a state of peace and surrender. When we allow ourselves to rest deeply, we give our bodies and minds the space to heal and recharge. Restfulness restores balance, calming the mind's chatter and reconnecting us to our natural rhythm. When we genuinely honor what our body is telling us, by surrendering to what our inner wisdom may be asking—we may find that 'deep rest' is an essential part of healing and awakening.

Today, give yourself permission to rest. Set aside time to breathe, reflect, and simply be. Perhaps, take a few days off and simply relax into deep rest. Rest is not a luxury but often a necessity for well-being and growth.

I honor restfulness, trusting in the power of stillness to restore.

Truth (Knowing, not Believing)

Truth is not something imposed by others but a deep knowing that arises from within. It goes beyond belief systems and mental concepts, guiding us through direct experience. When we are present with life and listen to our intuition, truth reveals itself clearly and effortlessly.

Today, reflect on a truth you feel deeply, beyond external influence. Allow yourself to trust this inner knowing and let it guide you. Truth doesn't require validation—it simply is.

I connect with the truth within,
trusting the clarity of direct knowing.

Joy

J oy is a natural state that arises when we are fully alive and present. In fact, JOY is your essential nature that needs no reason. It doesn't depend on external achievements or possessions but on the simple experience of being as you already are. Practically speaking, joy invites us to celebrate life's small wonders, from a deep breath to a moment of laughter with a friend—everything!

Today, open your heart to joy that is already here now, regardless of circumstance or what the mind is saying. Notice the moments that bring a smile to your face and let them expand. Joy is always available when you choose to embrace it, notice it.

I welcome joy as a natural expression of my being.
Joy is what I already AM!

Beauty

B eauty is all around us, waiting to be noticed. It can be found in the colors of a sunset, the kindness of a stranger, birds singing their morning praises, or the gentle movement of a breeze. When we attune ourselves to beauty, we open our hearts to a deeper appreciation of life's richness.

Today, seek out beauty in unexpected places. Allow yourself to marvel at the intricate details of the world around you. Let beauty remind you of the sacredness of existence. You may choose to stare at yourself in the mirror until you become aware of the infinite beauty that you already are...always!

I open my eyes and heart to the beauty that surrounds me;
the infinite beauty that I already am.

Nature

Nature is a reflection of life's wisdom and harmony. The cycles of growth, rest, and renewal remind us that we too are part of this flow. By connecting with nature, we reconnect with our inner balance, the essence of all life—the real YOU—and find guidance in its quiet, steady presence.

Today, spend time in nature. Observe how it moves effortlessly—trees swaying in the wind, water flowing without resistance. Allow nature's presence to ground and inspire you. Notice that you ARE nature itSELF.

I am deeply connected to nature's wisdom and harmony. I AM nature!

Allowing Feelings and Emotions

Feelings and emotions arise naturally, yet we often spend our energy resisting them—believing that certain emotions should not be here, that they are too much, too uncomfortable, or somehow *wrong*. But emotions are not obstacles to get rid of; they are part of the natural flow of experience.

When we allow emotions to be as they are, without trying to fix, change, or suppress them, we free ourselves from inner conflict. We stop making an enemy of our own experience and instead become present with what is *actually* happening within us. This simple shift—from resistance to allowance—from avoidance to welcoming—creates space for emotions to move through us, rather than getting stuck inside. We even question happiness and peace, as if they shouldn't be here.

Today, notice your feelings and emotions as they arise, regardless if they feel positive or negative, instead of pushing it away, try saying: I allow you to be here. I welcome your presence. You are safe. Notice what happens when you meet your feelings, sensations, and emotions with openness instead of resistance.

I lovingly welcome and allow my feelings and emotions to move through this body with ease, knowing they are part of my natural experience.

Dis-identifying with Experience

We often believe we are the sum of our experiences—the body we inhabit, the thoughts we think, the emotions we feel. Yet, beyond these temporary states is a deeper, unchanging presence that simply observes. Dis-identifying with experience doesn't mean rejecting it; rather, it's recognizing that we are not limited to the roles, labels, identities, or sensations we temporarily experience.

Today, take a moment to sit in stillness and lovingly observe your thoughts and feelings as they arise. Notice how they come and go, like waves on the surface of the ocean, while the deeper part of you—the observer—remains unchanged.

I am not the body. I am not even the mind.

Unconditional

Unconditional love and acceptance invite us to embrace life without placing limits or requirements on it. To live unconditionally is to let go of expectations—of how things should be or how others should behave. It is the practice of meeting each moment, thought, and feeling with openness, allowing both ourselves and others to simply be.

Today, practice unconditional acceptance. Notice where you may be placing unnecessary conditions on your happiness, resisting or judging your feelings, or others' actions. Release those expectations and open your heart to what is present—life—infinitely and lovingly unfolding through and as everything.

I embrace life with unconditional love and acceptance of experience.

Yoga

Yoga is not just a physical practice but a way of harmonizing body, mind, and spirit. It invites us to connect with the present moment—to yourSELF—through movement, breath, and awareness. Yoga teaches balance between: effort and ease, strength and surrender, both on and off the mat. Yoga actually means Union—the union already here.

Today, engage in a moment of mindful movement or stillness. Whether through a yoga pose, a deep breath, or quiet reflection, let yourself feel the union of body and presence.

I align with the harmony of body, mind, and
spirit through the practice of yoga.

Humor

Humor lightens the heart and reminds us not to take life too seriously. It helps us see the absurdities in our struggles, bringing perspective and relief. True humor, rooted in joy rather than cynicism or sarcasm, connects us to others and lifts our spirit in challenging moments.

Today, find humor in the small things. Allow yourself to laugh, even at your own mistakes, and notice how humor creates space for joy and connection.

I welcome humor into my life, allowing it to lift my spirit.

Laugh

A good laugh is like a deep breath for the soul. It releases tension, shifts our energy, and brings us into the present moment. Laughter is contagious—spreading joy to those around us. When we laugh, we reconnect with the playful, light-hearted essence of life.

Today, give yourself permission to laugh freely. Whether with a friend, at a story, or simply at life's quirky moments, let laughter flow. Notice how it refreshes your mind and body.

I laugh with joy, bringing light and playfulness into my day.

Opening

Opening is an act of courage and trust. It invites us to release fear and control, allowing ourselves to be vulnerable and receptive to the flow of life. When we open our hearts and minds, we create space for deeper connection, growth, and transformation.

Today, reflect on where you may be closed off. What would happen if you allowed yourself to open more fully? Trust that opening to life brings new opportunities and experiences that support your highest good.

I open my heart to life, trusting in its unfolding
with compassionate courage and infinite grace.

MARCH 19

Appreciation

Appreciation brings us into direct connection with the present moment. When we take the time to appreciate the people, experiences, our feelings, sensations, and beauty around us, we cultivate a deeper sense of gratitude and joy. Appreciation helps us shift from lack to abundance, enriching our perspective on life.

Today, pause to appreciate something or someone in your life, even unsettling feelings. Let that appreciation fill you with warmth and presence. Notice how it deepens your connection to life's wonders and the absolute perfection of experience; whatever arises.

I cultivate appreciation, honoring the beauty and gifts in every moment.

MARCH 20

Prayer

Prayer is not only a request for help; it is a communion with the sacred, a moment of connection to something greater than the egoic mind. Whether through words, silence, or intention, prayer grounds us in humility, trust, and openness. It is a symbolic gesture to the mystery of the universe and reminds us that we are never truly apart from the source of all creation.

Today, offer a simple prayer. It may be for guidance, gratitude, or peace. Let the act of prayer connect you to the sacred presence within and around you.

I open my heart in prayer, trusting in the
presence of divine support and guidance.

Watching

To watch is to witness life without interference or judgment. It is the practice of observing thoughts, emotions, situations, and experiences as they arise and pass, allowing us to see clearly without attachment. Through this practice, we become more present and connected to the truth of the moment. In some religious context, this could be called, "Practicing the Presence of God."

Today, practice watching your inner and outer world. Observe your thoughts and feelings without trying to change them. Notice how this creates space for awareness, insight, and ease.

I watch with presence and openness,
trusting in the wisdom of awareness. I AM.

Gentleness

Gentleness is a quality of grace and tender loving care that softens life's rough edges, those rigid walls of defense and protection we have seemingly built around the heart. When we approach ourselves and others with gentleness, we nurture healing, connection, and trust. Gentleness invites us to release harsh judgments and meet life with an open, compassionate heart.

Today, practice gentleness in your thoughts, actions, and words. Be kind to yourself and others, knowing that gentleness is a powerful form of strength that heals and dissolves whatever is no longer serving you.

I embrace gentleness as a guiding presence in my life.

Doubtless

To be doubtless is not about rigid certainty but about trusting deeply in yourSELF and life's unfolding. It is the quiet confidence that arises when you are grounded in presence, knowing that even the unknown holds opportunities for growth. When doubt falls away, trust...and conscious clarity remains.

Today, reflect on where doubt may be holding you back. Don't believe those thoughts, for they are only thoughts. Lean into trust and take a step forward without hesitation? Allow doubtlessness to anchor you in peace and assurance that ALL IS WELL!

I trust myself and life's path, moving forward
with confidence and ease. All is WELL!

Nothing is That Big of a Deal

Often, we magnify problems in our minds, making them seem bigger than they are. When we step back and shift our perspective, we then see that many things aren't as overwhelming as they appeared. Letting go of unnecessary seriousness allows us to meet life with greater lightness and ease.

Today, when a challenge arises, pause and ask yourself: "Is this really that big of a deal?" Give yourself permission to breathe, smile, and let go of tension. Really, nothing is that big of a deal when you see it for what it is.

I release unnecessary seriousness and welcome
ease and gracefulness into my day.

MARCH 25

Playfulness

Playfulness connects us to our inner child—our inner wonder and awe of life—the part of us that delights in discovery, laughter, and creativity. It breaks through rigidity and invites spontaneity and joy. When we approach life with a sense of play, even challenges can become opportunities for learning and growth.

Today, invite playfulness into your life. Try something fun, creative, or unexpected. Let yourself be free of self-judgment and enjoy the moment.

I embrace playfulness, allowing joy and creativity
to flow through me—as ME.

MARCH 26

Clarity

Clarity arises when we remove the distractions and doubts clouding our higher vision toward inner and collective well-being. It is the ability to see things as they are, without distortion or confusion. Conscious clarity often comes through stillness—by listening to our inner wisdom and allowing truth to reveal itself naturally. Not by force, but by effortless trust in this-here-now—ever present grace.

Today, take a moment and open to conscious clarity. Breathe deeply and focus on what is truly important. Let go of mental clutter and trust in the wisdom that arises in stillness and serenity.

*I embrace clarity, allowing truth and
conscious purpose to guide my actions.*

Sustenance

Sustenance is what nourishes and supports us—physically, emotionally, and spiritually. When we are mindful of how we sustain ourselves, we cultivate balance and well-being. True sustenance comes from aligning with what genuinely fulfills and nurtures us; not just physically, but emotionally.

Today, reflect on what sustains you. Are there ways you can nourish yourself more fully—through rest, connection, disregarding hateful thoughts and embracing loving ones, or creativity? Honor the sources of sustenance in your life.

I nurture myself by embracing what sustains and uplifts me.

Earth

Earth is our physical foundation, offering stability, nourishment, and grounding. It supports all life, providing a steady presence beneath our feet; from the topsoil that feeds our food source to being the playground for all beings to freely express. By connecting to the earth, we cultivate a sense of rootedness and belonging, reminding ourselves of the interconnected web of life.

Today, spend time connecting with the earth. Take off your shoes and walk in the grass. Feel the ground beneath you. Notice the plants and trees, and express and feel gratitude for the life it supports. Put your hands in the soil and say, "Thank you." Let the earth's presence ground the body-mind.

I am grounded and nourished by the sacred presence of the earth.

Breathe

The breath is a constant companion, a bridge between body and mind. It anchors us to the present moment, offering a natural rhythm of renewal in every moment. By bringing awareness to your breath, you create space for calm clarity and balance; resting attention there.

Today, take moments to breathe deeply and mindfully. Let each breath remind you of the gift of life and the power of presence.

I connect to the present moment through the rhythm of my breath.

MARCH 30

Vitality

Vitality is the energy of life flowing through you. It is readily apparent when body, mind, and spirit are aligned by nurturing yourself with rest, movement, and conscious clarity. Vitality fuels creativity, joy, and confidence, empowering you to engage with life fully, happily, consciously—as life itSELF.

Today, reflect on what energizes and uplifts you. Are there habits that drain your vitality? Take a small step to support your life-force through nourishment, movement, or rest. Embrace vitality now.

I nurture my vitality by aligning with the flow of life within me—as ME.

Family

Family, whether chosen or given, is a source of deep connection and belonging. It is within these relationships that we learn, grow, and experience both challenges and profound love. Healthy family relationships are built on mutual respect, care, and forgiveness, offering us opportunities for healing, genuine connection, and grace.

Today, reflect on the role of family in your life, whether it is a support group family, friends, or those who raised you. Are there relationships that could benefit from more understanding or care? Reach out to someone you consider family and offer a moment of connection. Remember, we are all part of the ONE Human Family.

I honor the bonds of family, nurturing connection
and understanding. Everyone is my family.

APRIL 1

Potential

Within each of us lies infinite potential. It unfolds as we learn, grow, and embrace new experiences. Often, our greatest limitations come from beliefs we place on ourselves. By releasing these self-imposed boundaries, we allow our potential to expand beyond what we thought possible.

Today, reflect on the areas where you might be holding yourself back. What new possibilities can you open yourself to? Trust that your potential is always evolving and waiting to be discovered.

I embrace the infinite potential within,
allowing it to unfold with trust and loving curiosity.

APRIL 2

Feeling

Feelings are the language of the soul, offering guidance and insight into your inner world. When you allow yourself to fully feel without judgment, you create space for healing and transformation. Suppressed emotions can block your energy, while allowing them to flow brings clarity and balance.

Today, tune into your feelings by scanning your body with kind and curious loving attention. Notice what arises without labeling it as good or bad - OR - right or wrong. Notice that feelings cannot harm you. Allow yourself to fully experience your emotions, trusting that each feeling has a (non mental) message to offer.

I honor and embrace my feelings, allowing them to guide and heal.

Honoring

To honor is to recognize the sacredness in yourself, others, and life itself. Honoring invites us to approach each moment with reverence and gratitude, allowing ourselves and others to have authentic experience, letting life be as it is. When we honor our journey, we acknowledge our struggles and triumphs as essential parts of our growth.

Today, reflect on how you can honor yourself and those around you. Whether through words, actions, or moments of presence, offer respect and gratitude for the sacredness in all.

I honor the sacredness within myself, others,
and the experiences that shape my life.

Healing

Healing is a process of awakening to the wholeness that never left. It requires patience, compassion, and a willingness to face what needs care and attention; gently peeling back the apparent layers of pain, hurt, and unattended sorrow. Healing often occurs in phases, revealing deeper truths as we release old wounds and embrace new strength and expression.

Today, offer yourself a moment of healing. Whether through rest, reflection, or a gentle action, trust that you are capable of nurturing your own well-being. Healing is not linear—each seeming step, whenever it arrives, matters, and has a purpose for you to discover.

I open myself to healing, allowing peace, renewal,
and conscious clarity to flow through me.

Divine Feminine

The Divine Feminine embodies qualities of intuition, nurturing, creativity, and flow. It is also the essence of receptivity that allows us to open our hearts and minds to the kind and tender lovingness that pervades all of existence. Divine Feminine energy is the soft yet powerful force that nurtures life and guides us through cycles of rest and renewal. By honoring this aspect of the life-force within, we become aware of our natural wisdom, compassion, and capacity to create and care for all of the Universe's creations.

Today, tune into the qualities of the Divine Feminine within you. Allow intuition, receptivity, and gentleness to guide your thoughts and actions. Embrace your connection to the sacred cycles of life.

I honor the Divine Feminine within, embracing intuition, compassion, creativity, and ability to receive tender love.

This Here Now

The present moment is all we ever truly have. When we are fully here and now (which is always the case), we let go of regrets about the past and worries about the future. Presence connects us to peace, clarity, and the deep aliveness of life. It reminds us that everything we seek is already here within us—as us.

Today, practice bringing your attention to this infinite timeless and formless moment of herenow. Notice your breath, sensations, and surroundings. Feel your feet, grounded to the Earth. Allow yourself to rest fully in the here and now, free from distraction.

I rest in the sacred presence of this here now, fully alive and aware.

Infinite-ness

The essence of life is infinite—without boundaries or limitations; even beyond the illusion of time. Beneath the surface of our thoughts and experiences lies a vast, ever-present eternal loving awareness that transcends time and form. When we somehow let go of the illusion of disconnection with our infinite essence, we release the constraints of fear and scarcity, realizing that we are part of an endless flow of creation and possibility. And infinitely abundant. That what "I" really "AM" is the infinite ever-present loving awareness from which all experience arises.

Today, reflect on the infinite nature of your being. Imagine the limitless potential within you and trust in life's boundless possibilities.

I am ALREADY connected to the infinite essence of life, beyond all limitations. I AM the infinite UNIVERSE!

Discernment

Discernment is the ability to see clearly, choosing what aligns with your truth and highest good. It is not about judgment but about making thoughtful choices guided by wisdom and intuition. Discernment allows you to move through life with clarity, knowing which paths to take and which to release. It helps you recognize when something is nourishing or depleting, authentic or misleading, expansive or limiting. Without discernment, we may follow habits, expectations, or external pressures that do not serve us. With it, we navigate life with greater purpose, integrity, and alignment.

Today, practice discernment in your decisions. Pause and reflect before acting. Trust your inner knowing to guide you toward choices that support your well-being and growth. Notice how it feels to act from wisdom rather than impulse.

I trust my discernment to guide me with clarity and wisdom.

Pause

Pausing is a powerful act of presence. In a world that moves quickly, taking a moment to pause allows us to reconnect with ourselves as the present moment. Through pausing, we can release tension, reflect with clarity, and choose our next steps with greater intention, conscious clarity, and grace.

Today, give yourself permission to pause. Whether during moments of stress or reflection, take a deep breath and allow yourself to simply be. Notice how pausing restores balance and calm.

I honor the power of pause, allowing myself space to rest, consciously breathe, and reflect; even in a busy environment.

Confidence

True confidence arises from self-trust. It is not about being perfect or knowing all the answers but about trusting in your ability to navigate life's challenges. Confidence is cultivated by showing up fully and embracing your unique strengths and imperfections alike. At a visceral level, confidence is about befriending your feelings and sensations, and knowing that they are nothing to be afraid of. They are merely the play of life unfolding through the body-mind organism. You are the confident watcher of feelings. The observer of thoughts.

Today, reflect on your strengths and past accomplishments.

Trust in your natural loving and compassionately loving wisdom to handle whatever comes your way. And, bring to mind the countless times when you believed your feelings would never end; yet they always do. Allow your compassionate confidence to befriend all aspects of experience.

I trust myself and face life with confidence and compassionate courage.
I allow all feelings and thoughts to be as they are.

APRIL 11

So What?

There are moments when we attach too much importance to small worries or perceived failures. Asking, "So what?" (not hatefully or dismissively, but compassionately) helps release unnecessary pressure and seriousness. It's a reminder that many things we stress over aren't as significant as we make them out to be. Letting go brings lightness and conscious perspective.

Today, if you feel overwhelmed by a situation, in a compassionate attitude of surrender, ask yourself: "So what?" Notice how this question can help you lovingly detach and see things more clearly.

I release unnecessary pressure and
embrace a sense of ease and graceful perspective.

APRIL 12

Friendship

Friendship is a sacred bond that nourishes the soul. True friends offer support, understanding, and joy, walking alongside us through life's highs and lows. Friendship thrives on trust, authenticity, and mutual care, creating a space where we can be fully ourselves.

Today, reflect on the friendships that enrich your life. Reach out to someone who has supported you and express gratitude for their presence.

*I cherish the gift of friendship, offering and
receiving love and connection.*

APRIL 13

Softness

Softness is a strength often misunderstood. It allows us to approach life and others with gentleness and compassion, breaking through barriers of fear and resistance, dominance and aggression. Softness doesn't mean weakness—it means meeting life with a tender, open heart.

Today, practice softness in your thoughts and actions. Offer yourself and others kindness and understanding. Notice how softness creates space for healing and connection.

*I embrace the strength of softness, nurturing peace
and compassion in my life.*

APRIL 14

Uncovering

Uncovering is the process of revealing the truth beneath layers of conditioning and illusion. As we peel back these layers, we reconnect with our authentic selves and the deeper wisdom that has always been within us. This process invites both courage and patience, as each discovery brings new conscious clarity.

Today, reflect on what you might be ready to uncover. What

truths or insights have been waiting for your kind, gentle, and loving attention? Allow yourself to move through this process with openness and trust.

I uncover the truth within, trusting the process of self-discovery.

Honest Questioning

Honest questioning is a practice of seeking truth through genuine curiosity and heartfelt reflection. It involves asking deep, meaningful questions about our beliefs, assumptions, and experiences. By questioning and examining our inner world with an open mind, we invite greater conscious clarity and compassionate understanding to permeate our lives, freeing ourselves from limiting patterns and habits no longer serving well-being.

Today, ask yourself a question that invites introspection, such as "What do I truly want?" or "What belief no longer serves me?" or "What feelings am I avoiding by acting out?" Be willing to tenderly sit with the question and allow insights to emerge naturally.

I engage in honest questioning, inviting clarity and truth into my life.

Creativity

Creativity is the expression of life's energy flowing through you. It is not limited to art or performance but appears in countless ways—through problem-solving, new ideas, and acts of imagination. When you embrace creativity, you allow yourself to co-create with life as life itSELF, discovering new perspectives and possibilities.

Today, engage in a creative act. Let go of self-judgment and allow your natural curiosity to guide you. Creativity thrives when you give it space to play and explore.

*I honor my creative essence, allowing life to flow
through me in new and inspiring ways.*

APRIL 17

Vulnerability

Vulnerability is the courage to be seen and known, even in moments of uncertainty or discomfort. It opens the door to deeper connection, trust, and authenticity. Though it can feel risky, vulnerability ultimately empowers us to live fully, free from the masks we often wear. Free from the burdens of trying to be someone we are not. Through vulnerability we find our true invulnerability.

Today, reflect on where you might be holding back from vulnerability, from authenticity, from simply "being as you are." Can you share your truth with someone you trust? Allow yourself to be open and seen, knowing that vulnerability is a strength.

*I embrace vulnerability, allowing myself
to be open, real, and fully present.*

APRIL 18

Joyful Irony

Life is full of paradoxes and playful twists that invite us to laugh at ourselves and the unexpected. Joyful irony helps us see the humor in situations that may first appear frustrating. It reminds us not to take life too seriously and to embrace the beauty of life's unpredictability, awe, and surprise in every moment.

Today, look for moments of joyful irony. Where can you find

humor and delight in the twists of life's unfolding? Let yourself laugh and be uplifted by life's surprises.

I embrace joyful irony, welcoming humor and lightness into my life.

Forgiving-ness

Forgiving-ness is the act of releasing the heavy burden of judgment—for 'giving' ourselves a loving break from self-judgment and judging others. It is not about excusing harm but about giving ourselves permission to let go and heal. When we give ourselves a break from judging, resentment dissolves, opening the door to everlasting peace and compassion.

Today, reflect on how you may be judging yourself or others, and acknowledge with loving kindness the irony of believing "judgment" is somehow beneficial. Offer gentle compassion, knowing that giving the mind a break from judging is a gift of liberation for your heart. True grace.

I release self-judgment and offer myself and
others the gift of forgiving-ness.

Connectedness

Connectedness reminds us that we are never truly separate. Every being, every experience, is part of an intricate web of life. When we open our hearts to this reality, we cultivate compassion, empathy, and a sense of belonging. True connection nourishes both the giver and the receiver, deepening our understanding of ourselves. Knowing that we are both the giver and receiver always, simultaneously.

Today, reflect on your connections—to people, nature, and your experience of feelings, emotions, and sensations. How can you strengthen these connections through presence and care?

I honor the deep connectedness that unites all of life.

Inspiration

Inspiration breathes life into our dreams and aspirations into our ability to create and freedom to express. It often arrives when we least expect it—through nature, art, or the wisdom of others. Inspiration uplifts and energizes us, awakening creativity and purpose. By staying open to inspiration, we invite new possibilities and ideas to flow into our lives.

Today, notice sources of inspiration. Pay attention to what sparks curiosity and excitement within you, and allow yourself to embrace them.

I open myself to the flow of inspiration, trusting it to guide my path.

Justice

Justice seeks balance, fairness, and integrity; not from our biased judgments and conditioned opinions; but from the deepest and most loving part of us that naturally knows beyond belief what true justice is. It honors the dignity and rights of all beings, advocating for truth and equity. True justice is not fueled by anger or vengeance but by compassionate commitment to allow harmony to prevail in the world.

Today, reflect on how you can contribute to greater justice in your life and community; not from necessarily thinking, but from feeling; receiving answers from the heart, not the head. Are there ways you can support fairness and inclusion for yourself and others?

I allow and embrace true justice to arise
with compassion, integrity, and respect for all.

Perspective

Perspective shapes how we experience life. By stepping outside of our immediate thoughts and emotions, we can see situations from a broader view. Perspective allows us to be more interested in understanding than remaining attached to being understood. This shift helps us release attachment to temporary struggles and discover new possibilities. Expanding our perspective often brings greater clarity, compassionate understanding, and peace.

Today, notice where you may be stuck in a narrow viewpoint. How might the situation look from another perspective? Allow yourself to explore a new way of seeing.

I open myself to new perspectives, gaining insight and wisdom.

Integrating

Integration is the process of bringing all seemingly separate parts of our experience into harmony. So often, we live fragmented—our minds pulling in one direction, our emotions in another, our bodies carrying burdens we have yet to acknowledge. True well-being arises when we allow all aspects of ourselves—body, mind, and spirit—to align in a unified flow.

Integration does not mean forcing wholeness; it means allowing it. It is about embracing all parts of our experience, even those we once resisted. When we stop fighting within ourselves, life begins to feel more fluid, more connected, more whole. This is not just for our own well-being but for the collective harmony of all life.

Today, take a deep breath and invite integration. Let your mind, heart, and body come into balance. Allow yourself to move with life, rather than against it.

I welcome the process of integration, allowing all
parts of experience to come into harmony.

APRIL 25

Neutrality

Neutrality is the ability to hold space for all sides without judgment. It does not mean indifference but rather an open-hearted awareness that allows clarity and fairness, genuinely compassionate understanding. Neutrality helps us stay centered and grounded, even in emotionally charged situations.

Today, practice neutrality by observing your thoughts and emotions without immediately reacting. Notice how this creates space for deeper understanding and insight—inner peace.

I cultivate neutrality, allowing myself to respond with calm and clarity.

APRIL 26

Primal Innocence

Innocence is the pure, unconditioned part of ourselves that remains open, curious, and full of wonder. It is not ignorance but a trust in life's unending beauty and infinite goodness. When we connect with our primal innocence that is always here as our true nature, we rediscover the joy of being fully present and alive, fearlessly unguarded.

Today, allow yourself to see the world with fresh eyes. Approach life with curiosity and awe, letting go of preconceived notions.

I reconnect with my inner primal innocence, welcoming joy and wonder.

APRIL 27

Earnestness

Earnestness is the sincerity and dedication we bring to our intentions and efforts; especially our spiritual practice. It is the quality of approaching life with depth, focus, and compassionate one-pointedness toward well-being. Earnestness invites us to fully commit to our highest path, trusting that our efforts will bear fruit in time.

Today, reflect on something that matters deeply to you. How can you approach it with sincerity and presence with your full attention? Let earnestness guide your actions with willingness and trust.

I bring earnestness to my path, honoring
my deepest values and intentions.

APRIL 28

Lightness

Life often invites us to embrace lightness—a playful, gentle approach that softens difficulties and uplifts the spirit. Lightness is not about dismissing challenges but about holding them with grace and non judgmental perspectives. When we release heaviness and obsessive thinking, we allow space for joy and ease to naturally arise.

Today, invite lightness into your life. Smile, laugh, and allow yourself to release any tension you may be carrying. Notice how this shifts your energy and outlook.

I embrace lightness, allowing joy and ease to flow through me. As ME.

APRIL 29

Gratefulness

Gratefulness is a beautiful form of gratitude, rooted in an appreciation for all of life's experiences. It acknowledges both the gifts and challenges as opportunities for growth and transformation. When we live with gratefulness, we become more present and attuned to life's abundance, and the graceful presence we are.

Today, reflect on the moments and people you are grateful for and allow yourself to see everything with loving eyes. Let that feeling fill your heart and guide your actions. At a deeper level, you may allow yourself to be grateful for all feelings, sensations, and emotions, regardless of the meaning you attach to them; regardless of how they feel. They are perfectly whole and okay as they are. All experiences are a gift of life.

I live as the essence of gratefulness,
honoring the richness of each moment.

APRIL 30

Response-ability

Response-ability is the power to consciously respond to life's circumstances rather than reacting unconsciously. It arises when we cultivate awareness, allowing us to choose actions that align with

our values and intentions—for the well-being of all. By embracing response-ability, we reclaim our autonomy and inner strength to be the conscious change we wish to see in the world.

Today, notice moments where you feel triggered or reactive. Pause, breathe, and choose how you wish to respond. Trust in your ability to meet life with serene awareness and mature intention.

I embrace my response-ability, choosing consciously loving actions in every moment.

MAY 1

Patience

Patience is the quiet strength that allows us to endure and grow through life's challenges. It teaches us to trust in timing, knowing that all things unfold as they are meant to. Patience invites us to release urgency and find peace in merely "trusting the process;" no matter how challenging or uplifting.

Today, practice patience with yourself and others. Notice where you may be rushing or forcing an outcome. Allow yourself to surrender to the flow of life.

I cultivate patience, trusting in life's natural unfolding.
I trust the process of life.

MAY 2

Quietness

Quietness is a space of deep rest and reflection. In the stillness, we reconnect with our inner wisdom and find peace beyond the noise of the mind. Quietness allows us to recharge, listen, and be present with what truly matters—this-here-now.

Today, create a moment of quietness in your day. Turn inward, breathe deeply, and listen to the presence within you. Let this quietness restore and guide you.

I honor the gift of quietness,
finding peace and wisdom within.

MAY 3

Universal Loving Force

Within each of us resides the power to restore conscious clarity and well-being. This power is not separate from life but deeply connected to the Universal Loving Force that flows through all existence. When we open to this possibility, we discover that we can draw on this force as qualities like trust, compassion, gratitude, diligent focus, and willingness. By nurturing these inner strengths and allowing ourselves to receive external support when needed, we find the compassionate fortitude to navigate life's challenges with grace.

Today, reflect on how you can connect with the Universal Loving Force within you. Which inner quality—trust, compassion, gratitude—do you feel called to embody today? Allow this connection to guide and sustain you.

I open as the Universal Loving Force,
trusting in my inner strength and clarity.

MAY 4

Nourishment

Nourishment is essential for all aspects of life—physical, emotional, and spiritual. It goes beyond food and drink, encompassing the relationships, experiences, and practices that sustain and energize us. True nourishment brings balance and vitality, reminding us to care for ourselves with kindness and intention. Just as the body requires wholesome food, the heart needs love, the mind or soul needs inspiration and stillness. Nourishment is about what we consume—not just physically, but mentally and emotionally. The words we hear, the environments we immerse ourselves in, and the energy we surround ourselves with all contribute to our well-being.

Today, reflect on what truly nourishes you. Are there areas of your life that need more care and attention? Allow yourself to receive the nourishment you need to thrive, and intentionally choose what uplifts and sustains you.

I honor my need for nourishment, caring for
myself with love and intention.

MAY 5

You-niverse

You are not separate from the universe—you are the universe. Every being, every experience, is the universe expressing itself in infinite diversity. When you recognize this, you realize that you are deeply connected to all that exists. The vastness of life flows through you, and you are an essential part of its unfolding.

Today, reflect on your connection to the universe. How does your inner world reflect the greater whole? Embrace the truth that you are both a unique individual and the universe itself in motion.

I am the universe in expression, deeply connected to all of life.

MAY 6

Wisdom

Wisdom arises from experience, reflection, and deep listening. Unlike knowledge, which is acquired from outside sources, wisdom comes from within. It often reveals itself when we quiet the mind and allow intuition to guide us. Wisdom helps us navigate life with clarity and purpose, offering insights that align with our highest truth.

Today, create space for wisdom to emerge. Take time to reflect on a challenge you're facing and listen to the quiet knowing within. Trust that the answers you seek are already present.

I trust in the wisdom within me to
guide my path with clarity and truth.

Assurance

Assurance is the deep trust that life is unfolding as it should—rather, as it already is, perfectly. It does not mean all challenges will vanish but that you have the strength and support to face them. Assurance arises from self-trust and faith in the greater flow of life, allowing you to meet uncertainty with calm and confidence from a deeper dimension of reality.

Today, offer yourself the gift of assurance. Reflect on how life has carried you through difficulties before. Trust in your ability to move forward with compassionate courage and everlasting grace.

I trust in the unfolding of life and find
assurance in my inner strength as grace itSELF.

Water

Water is one of the sacred elements that sustains all life. It flows effortlessly, adapting to its surroundings, yet it has immense power to transform landscapes over time. Water teaches us the importance of flexibility, nourishment, and renewal. It invites us to let go of resistance and move with life's natural rhythms.

Today, reflect on the presence of water in your life. Drink mindfully, appreciating its life-giving energy. Allow water's wisdom to remind you to flow with grace and adaptability.

I honor the sacred element of water,
allowing its flow to inspire and sustain me.

MAY 9

Faith

Faith is a trust in the unseen, a knowing that life holds greater wisdom than we can always understand. It is not blind belief but a deep sense of knowingness and trust that even in uncertainty, we are somehow supported. Faith allows us to surrender fear and embrace life's unfolding with openness.

Today, reflect on an area of your life where you could embrace faith—trusting the mystery of life to handle it. Can you release control and trust that life will guide you? Allow faith to anchor you in moments of uncertainty.

I trust in the greater wisdom of life, embracing faith as a guiding force.

MAY 10

It's Okay, Already.

Often we place unnecessary pressure on ourselves, holding onto perfectionism or the belief that things aren't good enough; or even believing "I'm not worthy." But life often whispers the reminder: It's okay, already. And, you are naturally worthy already because you are a perfect life, no matter what the mind says. You don't need to have all the answers or get everything right. By softening your expectations, you create space for peace and acceptance.

Today, give yourself permission to let go of unnecessary tension. Breathe deeply and affirm: It's okay, already. Trust that you are exactly where you need to be. And, that you are already enough.

I release the need for perfection and
embrace peace in the present moment.

MAY 11

Solitude

Solitude is not isolation; it is the conscious turning inward to find happiness, fulfillment, and wisdom from within. When we cultivate solitude, we step away from external distractions and reconnect with our true essence. It is a space where we can listen deeply to ourselves, nourish our spirit, and remember that lasting peace is not found outside of us but within.

Today, embrace a moment of solitude—not to escape, but to return home to yourself. Sit in quiet reflection, breathe deeply, and feel the richness of your own presence.

I honor solitude as a sacred space to discover peace,
fulfillment, and joy within myself.

MAY 12

Sacredness

Sacredness is not something found outside of us—it is the essence of who we are when we open our hearts and minds to our deepest truth. When we honor our most sacred qualities—love, kindness, wisdom, and presence—we nurture well-being in every sense. Sacredness is not reserved for certain places or moments; it is woven into everyday life, present in how we treat ourselves, others, and the world around us. By living from this sacred space, we bring healing and harmony to ourselves and the world around us, fostering deeper connection, understanding, and peace.

Today, reflect on what feels sacred within you. What qualities, when embraced, bring you the greatest sense of peace and fulfillment? How can you embody them more fully in your daily interactions? Allow these qualities to guide your thoughts, words, and actions, recognizing the sacred in all things.

I honor the sacredness within me, nurturing my well-being and sharing my light with the world.

MAY 13

Humility

Humility is not about diminishing ourselves or subjecting ourselves to indignant circumstance, but about seeing life with clear, open eyes, as it is. It is the quiet strength of recognizing that we are always learning, always growing, and always part of something greater than our self-images and self-concepts. Humility allows us to move through the world with gratitude, curiosity, and a willingness to listen—to ourselves, to others, and to life itself. To be aware.

Today, practice humility by embracing the wisdom of not knowing everything. Allow yourself to learn, to receive, and to see the beauty in all perspectives. True humility nurtures growth, connection, and deeper understanding.

I walk with humility, knowing that life is my greatest teacher.

Exuberance

Exuberance is the radiant expression of joy, enthusiasm, and vitality. It arises when we allow ourselves to fully embrace life, unburdened by fear or hesitation. This energy is contagious, uplifting not only ourselves but also those around us. When we give ourselves permission to be exuberant, we reconnect with the natural playfulness and wonder of being alive.

Today, allow yourself to express joy freely. Laugh, move, celebrate—even in the smallest of ways. Let your exuberance be a light that brightens your own path and the paths of others.

I embrace the exuberance of life, allowing joy
and energy to flow through me. As ME.

Harmony

Harmony is the natural state of balance that exists when we align with the flow of life. It is found in the spaces between sound and silence, action and stillness, giving and receiving. When we cultivate harmony within ourselves—through our thoughts, emotions, and actions—and by taking our kind and loving attention into the body to befriend our feelings and sensations, it radiates outward, creating peace in our relationships and the world around us.

Today, seek harmony in your day. Notice where balance is needed and gently adjust your focus, choices, and energy. Trust that life moves in rhythms, and you are part of its natural flow.

I cultivate harmony by aligning with the balance and flow of life.

Goodness

Goodness is not something to achieve but something to recognize—it is already present in every one of us and even in the world. In fact, goodness is the underlying essence of the human being when we let our guards down. It is reflected in the kindness of a stranger, the warmth of a smile, and the simple moments of care we offer to ourselves and others. When we nurture goodness, we amplify its presence, reminding ourselves that no act of kindness is too small to make a difference.

Today, take a moment to recognize the goodness around you. Express gratitude for it, and extend it through a kind word, a helping hand, or a moment of understanding.

I see and cultivate the goodness within myself and the world around me.

Support

Support is both the strength we offer others and the willingness to receive it when needed. It reminds us that we are not meant to walk alone—we thrive through connection, trust, and shared presence. True support is given with love, free from expectation, and received with gratitude, free from guilt.

Today, reflect on where you may need support and allow yourself to ask for or receive it with openness. Keep in mind, "No one can do it alone, yet no one can do it for you." Thus is the inseparable grace always available through the human being in this mystery of life.

I give and receive support with openness, knowing we are all connected.

Selfless Service

Selfless service is the act of giving from the heart, expecting nothing in return. It is an expression of unconditional love and compassion, recognizing that we are all interconnected, arising from the same inseparable source. When we serve selflessly, we step beyond ego-mind, allowing generosity and kindness to flow freely. This form of service not only uplifts others but also nourishes our own spirit.

Today, offer an act of service—big or small—with no expectation of recognition or reward. Let the act itself be enough, unconcerned with results, knowing that even the smallest gestures create endless ripples of kindness.

I serve with an open heart, honoring the deep
connection with all beings; as my very SELF.

Compassionate Courage

Compassionate courage is the bravery to act with kindness, even in the face of fear, uncertainty, or discomfort. It is the willingness to show up for others, to speak truth with love, and to meet life's challenges with an open heart. True courage is not hardened—it is softened by grace, allowing humble strength and compassionate understanding shine.

Today, embody compassionate courage. Whether through a difficult conversation, an act of self-care, or standing up for what is right, allow both bravery and kindness to guide your actions.

I move through life with compassionate courage,
allowing love and strength to guide me.

Befriending Experience

To befriend experience is to meet our feelings and sensations with gentle, compassionate curiosity. Instead of resisting or judging what arises in the body, we turn toward it with kindness, allowing each sensation to be acknowledged, understood, and honored. When we welcome our experience in this way, we soften the struggle and create space for healing and self-awareness. Prior to thought and mental interpretations of experience is the direct feeling-ness of life, the spontaneous felt sense of being alive. There are no right or wrong feelings and sensations. They are exactly as they are when we allow ourselves to befriend them.

Today, bring your attention to the feelings and sensations within your body. Whether pleasant or uncomfortable, meet them with curiosity rather than resistance. Breathe into them, offer them kindness, and allow yourself to fully be with what is.

I befriend experience with gentle awareness,
embracing each sensation with kindness and presence.

Invitation

Life is an ongoing invitation—to learn, to grow, to mature, and to awaken to the truth of our essential inseparable universal being. Every experience, whether joyful or challenging, offers an opportunity to deepen our awareness and understanding of what one really is. When we recognize life as an invitation to seek our infinite happiness and sense of self from within rather than an obstacle, we shift from resistance to acceptance, allowing transformation to unfold naturally.

Today, notice the invitations life is offering you. What lessons, insights, or awakenings are waiting in your current experiences? Approach each moment with openness, curiosity, and the willingness to grow.

I accept life's invitation to awaken, embracing each experience as an opportunity for growth and deeper understanding.

MAY 22

Letting Go

Letting go is an act of trust—releasing what no longer serves our well-being so that we can create space for what truly nourishes us. Whether it is an old belief, a habit, a past hurt, or an attachment to control, holding on can keep us stuck. Letting go does not mean losing or giving up; it means choosing freedom, allowing life to unfold with greater ease and clarity.

Today, reflect on what you may be holding onto that no longer supports your well-being. Breathe deeply, soften your grip, and allow yourself to release with trust.

I let go of what no longer serves me, creating space for peace, clarity, and new possibilities.

MAY 23

Divine Masculine

The Divine Masculine is not about gender—it is the cosmic yang energy that expresses strength, clarity, action, and presence. When in balance with the Divine Feminine, it guides with wisdom, protects without domination, and leads with integrity. The Divine

Masculine is the steady force that moves forward in harmony with life, acting not from ego but from deep alignment with universal truth.

Today, reflect on how the Divine Masculine energy expresses itself in your life. Are there areas where you can embody strength with gentleness, action with wisdom, or presence with purpose?

I allow the Divine Masculine within me to express itself with clarity, balanced strength, and integrity.

MAY 24

Space

Space is an essential gift we can offer ourselves and others. It allows for rest, healing, clarity, and growth. Just as a seed needs space to sprout and expand, we too need spaciousness in our minds, emotions, and relationships. When we create space, we open the door for transformation and new possibilities.

Today, notice where space may be helpful. Do you need a moment of stillness, room for creativity, or distance to gain perspective? Offer yourself that space, and honor the need for space in others as well.

I honor the liberating quality of space, allowing room for clarity, healing, and renewal.

MAY 25

Being

Being is the state of presence—beyond thought, beyond action, beyond striving. It is resting in awareness itself, free from the need to do or accomplish. When we surrender to simply being, we reconnect with our true nature, experiencing life as it unfolds effortlessly.

Today, allow yourself a moment of pure being. Sit in stillness, let go of the need to fix or achieve, and simply rest in the awareness of existence. Notice how peace naturally arises when you stop seeking and simply allow yourself to be.

I honor the sacredness of being, allowing myself
to rest in the fullness of the present moment.

MAY 26

Embracing

Embracing is the act of meeting life with openness and trust. It is saying yes to the next right thing, even when the path ahead is uncertain. To embrace is to move forward with trust or faith, releasing resistance and accepting what life is offering herenow.

Today, reflect on what life is asking you to embrace. What is the next right step that calls to you? Welcome it with an open heart, knowing that each step is leading you forward in the right direction no matter how difficult it may seem. It's okay.

I embrace the next right thing with trust,
allowing life to guide me. I am safe.

MAY 27

Asking

Asking is an act of courage and self-honoring. Whether we are asking for help, guidance, or clarity, we acknowledge our needs and trust that support is available to us. Asking does not make us weak; it deepens connection and reminds us that we are not meant to journey alone.

Today, practice asking for what you need. Whether it is help from a friend, wisdom from within, or guidance from the universe, allow yourself to reach out and receive.

I honor my needs by asking with openness and trust.

MAY 28

Dissolving

Dissolving is the gentle release of the egoic 'personal will' into the greater cosmic flow. It is the surrender of control, allowing ourselves to be carried by the vast intelligence of creation. When we dissolve the illusion of separateness, we align with the universal rhythm, moving in harmony with all that is.

Today, reflect on an area of life where you are holding on too tightly. Can you soften your grip, dissolve resistance, and allow life to unfold as it is meant to?

I surrender my personal will to the cosmic flow,
trusting in the wisdom of all creation.

MAY 29

Dance

Life is a dance—sometimes fluid and graceful, sometimes wild and unpredictable. The rhythm of life moves through us in every moment, inviting us to step into the flow with trust and joy. When we let go of self-consciousness and expectations, we allow ourselves to dance freely, unburdened by fear or hesitation.

Today, dance—literally or figuratively, like no one is watching. Move through your day with lightness, letting go of the need for perfection. Let go of the compulsion to please others. Just for today, give yourself permission to disappoint everyone...AND...DANCE. Trust in the rhythm of life, knowing that each step is part of a greater harmony.

I dance with life, embracing its rhythm with joy, trust, and freedom.

Abundance

Abundance is not just about having more—it is about seeing the fullness of what is already here. When we live in an attitude of abundance, we stop focusing on what we lack and begin recognizing the infinite richness of life. There is abundance in every breath, in the warmth of the sun, in the presence of love, in the ability to give and receive.

True abundance is not something to chase; it is a reality to *notice*. It exists beyond material wealth—it is the overflowing generosity of life itself. When we shift our attention to what is already present, we realize that we are never truly without.

Today, practice seeing abundance. Instead of asking, "What am I missing?" ask, "What is already here for me to appreciate?"

I embrace the abundance of life, knowing that
everything I need is already within and around me.

Turning to Inner Wisdom

There is a silent wisdom within, untouched by fear, conditioning, or restless thought. When we turn toward this deeper intelligence, we step away from compulsion and into conscious clarity. By trusting this inner guidance, our false identities dissolve, revealing the wholeness that has always been—free of personal identity.

Today, pause before reacting. Instead of being led by thought or habit, turn inward. Listen. Trust. Let your essential being emerge.

I trust the deeper wisdom within,
allowing clarity and wholeness to guide me.

JUNE 1

Sensitivity

Sensitivity is not weakness—it is the deepening of awareness, the ability to feel life more fully. As we heal, feel, and awaken, our sensitivity grows, allowing us to connect more deeply with ourselves, others, and the world. Rather than resisting it, we can embrace sensitivity as a natural part of our unfolding.

Today, honor your sensitivity. Instead of seeing it as something to suppress, recognize it as a gift—one that brings depth, connection, and presence.

I welcome my sensitivity as a natural
part of healing, feeling, and awakening.

JUNE 2

Meekness

Meekness is often misunderstood as weakness, but it is, in truth, quiet strength. It is the ability to move through life without arrogance, to be open rather than forceful, and to trust in life's unfolding without the need for control. Meekness allows us to surrender the false-self and rest in the natural wisdom of being.

Today, practice moving gently. Trust that true power comes not from force but from presence, humility, and openness.

I embrace meekness as strength,
allowing life to unfold with grace and trust.

JUNE 3

Enoughness

You are already enough—here, now, as you are. No achievement, validation, or improvement is required for your worth to be complete. The mind may tell stories of lacking or striving, but beneath those thoughts, your essential being remains whole and untouched. The mind may be thinking and believing it is unworthy, undeserving, and unwhole; but that is only the mind; not the reality of you as pure Loving Awareness. You do not have to prove yourself to anyone, not even yourself; because the REAL YOU is already, whole, complete, enough, just as you are.

Today, release the pressure to prove, fix, or become more. Instead, rest in the deep truth of your enoughness.

I am already enough, whole and complete right
here now, always and forever.

JUNE 4

Inseparable

You are not separate from life—you are life itself. Some people call the underlying reality and source of all creation, God. You are not separate from God. That is to say, there is no dividing line between you and the universe, between your being and the vast intelligence of existence. The illusion of separateness fades when we recognize that we are an inseparable expression of Reality, of God, of Cosmic Consciousness unfolding.

Today, feel into this truth. Notice how every breath, every sensation, every moment arises as part of the great inseparable whole.

I am inseparable from the universe, one with all that is. I AM.

Merging

There is a point where separation dissolves—where we no longer feel apart from life, love, or presence itself. Merging is not about losing ourselves but about dissolving the illusion of isolation and separation, realizing the already oneness as the flow of existence. It is the deep recognition that we are not outside of life looking in—we are life itself. Rumi wrote, "I have been knocking on heaven's door my entire life. The door opens. I have been knocking from inside." What you are seeking is already here now.

Today, notice where you are holding onto separateness. Can you soften into life, into presence, into the natural unfolding? Let yourself merge with the moment.

I release separation and merge with the flow of life,
trusting in my oneness with all.

Inwards

The world constantly calls us outward to distractions, validations, and endless activity. But the deepest truths, the greatest peace, and the most profound love are found by turning inwards. The source of unconditional love, the source of all existence is inside. When we quiet the noise and look within, we remember who we truly are beyond the surface of thoughts and identities.

Today, take a moment to turn inwards. Close your eyes, breathe, and rest in the silence within you. Let yourself watch thoughts without attaching to them. Notice the depth of your own presence.

I turn inwards, knowing that all I seek is already within.

Reality

Reality is not what the mind believes—it is what is. Beyond thought, beyond labels, beyond our interpretations, there is a raw, present truth unfolding in every moment. When we stop trying to impose meaning and simply experience life as it is, we open to a deeper, more honest way of being.

Today, observe reality without judgment. See, hear, and feel without labeling or resisting. What happens when you meet life just as it is prior to the mind's unnecessary interpretations and rationalizations?

I welcome reality as it is, free from illusion, mental noise, and resistance

Funny

Life is funny—not always in ways we expect, but in the way it unfolds with irony, surprises, and moments that remind us not to take ourselves too seriously. When we allow humor to soften our grip on perfection and control, we find lightness even in challenges. Laughter has the power to shift our perspective, to dissolve tension, and to remind us that life is not as rigid as we sometimes make it. Humor connects us, heals us, and keeps us present in the flow of life.

Today, let yourself laugh. Find humor in the unexpected, in your own quirks, in the way life plays out. Notice the absurdity, the unpredictability, and the beauty of it all. Joy is always waiting in the little moments—if you let it in.

I embrace the humor of life,
allowing laughter and lightness to uplift me.

Vision

Vision is more than seeing with the eyes—it is the ability to perceive beyond what is immediate, to sense possibility, and to trust in what has not yet fully unfolded. True vision arises from clarity, presence, and a deep inner knowing, guiding us toward alignment with our highest truth.

Today, take a moment to connect with your inner vision. What is life inviting you toward? Allow yourself to see beyond fear and limitation, trusting in the path ahead.

I trust in my inner vision,
allowing clarity and insight to guide me.

Receptivity

Receptivity is the art of openness—allowing life to come to us rather than forcing our way forward. When we soften into receptivity, we create space for insight, love, and guidance to flow in. It is through being open that we receive the support and wisdom already surrounding us. Everything we need is already herenow. We need only open our hearts and minds and listen with quiet joy—the everlasting Loving Awareness that we are.

Today, practice receptivity. Instead of striving, pause. Instead of trying to get ahead and outdo the other guy, listen. What is life offering you in this moment? Everything you are seeking is within. Allow yourself to receive.

I open myself to life,
trusting in the gifts that flow toward me.

Acknowledging Primal Innocence

Beneath all self-judgment, beyond every story the mind has told, there is a primal innocence—untouched, whole, and pure. Acknowledging this innocence allows us to see that we were never truly flawed, only conditioned to believe so. When we honestly examine the self-judgments we carry, we do so not to condemn ourselves, but to free ourselves.

Today, take a moment to recognize your innocence. Look at the judgments you have held against yourself with compassion, and ask—are they truly yours, or were they given to you?

I acknowledge my primal innocence,
releasing self-judgment with honesty and compassion.

Waking Up

Waking up is not a single moment but an ongoing unfolding—an awakening to the truth of who we are beyond conditioning, fear, and illusion. It is the willingness to see clearly, to meet life with awareness, and to recognize that we are not separate from the vast intelligence of existence. Each moment offers us the chance to wake up a little more.

Today, notice where you may be asleep in habit or thought. Can you bring fresh awareness to this moment? Let yourself wake up to what is real, here, now.

I welcome the ongoing awakening of my being,
seeing life with clarity and presence.

Dignity

Dignity is the quiet strength of knowing your worth, without needing validation from others or even yourself. It is not pride or superiority but an unwavering recognition of your inherent unconditional value. Everyone has infinite unconditional value simply because you exist. When we honor our natural value that no one can take away, we carry ourselves with dignity. We stand rooted in truth, unshaken by external opinions or circumstances.

Today, honor your unconditional value and dignity that does not need to be earned, achieved, or acquired. Walk with presence, speak with integrity, and trust in the depth of your being.

I embrace my dignity,
standing in the truth of my unconditional worth.

Wonder

Wonder is the ability to meet life with open eyes and an open heart—to see the ordinary as extraordinary. It is the spark of curiosity, the quiet awe in a sunset, the deep appreciation of life's intricate unfolding—grass growing, birds singing, bodies breathing. Wonder reminds us that we are not just here to understand life but to experience it fully.

Today, approach something familiar as if seeing it for the first time. Let yourself marvel at the miracle of simply being alive.

I embrace wonder, allowing life to
reveal its beauty anew in every moment.

Stillness

Stillness is not the absence of movement—it is the presence beneath it. In the depths of stillness, we find clarity, peace, and the quiet hum of existence itself. When we stop chasing, stop searching, and simply allow stillness to hold us, we remember what has always been here.

Today, take a moment of stillness. Let go of doing. Let go of thinking. Just be. Stillness speaks, not with words, but with insight.

I rest in stillness, allowing peace and presence to fill me.

Unencumbered

To be unencumbered is to move through life freely, without the weight of unnecessary burdens. We often carry beliefs, fears, and attachments that do not serve us, holding onto them out of habit. But when we release what is not essential, we discover a lightness—an openness to life as it is, unclouded by unnecessary struggle.

Today, notice what you are carrying that may no longer serve you. Can you let go, even just a little? Allow yourself to walk unencumbered.

I release what no longer serves me,
embracing the freedom of being unencumbered.

Friendliness

Friendliness is a warmth of spirit, a natural openness that connects us to others without fear or expectation. It is not just about being kind to those we know, but about carrying a gentle, welcoming presence wherever we go. When we approach life with friendliness, we create space for trust, ease, and shared humanity. We begin seeing everyone as our very SELF.

Today, bring friendliness into your interactions. Offer a smile, a kind word, or a moment of genuine presence. Notice how it transforms both you and the world around you.

I meet life and others with friendliness,
opening my heart to connection and warmth.

JUNE 18

Tranquility

Tranquility is the stillness that arises when we stop resisting life. It is not about eliminating challenges but about remaining at peace within them. True tranquility comes from accepting each moment as it is, knowing that no storm lasts forever.

Today, allow tranquility to settle within you. Take a deep breath, soften into the present, and trust that all is unfolding as it should.

I cultivate tranquility by embracing
the present moment with peace and trust.

JUNE 19

Okay-ness

There is a quiet power in realizing that, in this moment, everything is already okay. The mind may tell stories of struggle or lack, but beneath it all, there is a steady presence that remains untouched. When we stop striving for things to be different and accept what is, a deep okay-ness naturally emerges.

Today, practice okay-ness. No need to fix, push, or force—simply rest in the enough-ness of this moment.

I allow myself to be as I am,
knowing that this moment is already okay.

Without Concern

Love, when given freely, shines without attachment—without the need for recognition, reciprocation, or results. True love does not measure or control; it simply radiates, like the sun offering warmth without concern for who receives it. When we love without concern, we step into the purest form of giving, free from expectation or fear.

Today, let your love flow without concern. Offer kindness, presence, or warmth without waiting for a return. Let love be its own reason.

I allow love to radiate freely,
without concern for results, trusting in its natural flow.

JUNE 21

Non-Doing

Non-doing is the art of allowing life to unfold without grasping, controlling, or taking ownership of what arises. The body moves, the mind thinks, sensations come and go—yet beneath it all, there is a deeper presence that simply observes. When we rest in non-doing, we recognize that we are not the doer, but the awareness in which all experience unfolds.

Today, step back from the need to control. Watch thoughts and actions arise naturally, without claiming them as yours. Simply observe.

I rest in non-doing, allowing life to unfold effortlessly within awareness.

Conscious Admission

To consciously admit is to bring into the light what has long been hidden. When we acknowledge and admit our believed self-judgments—to our Universal Self, our personal self, and another—we see that these aspects are not separate but one and the same. In this openness, judgment loses its grip, and we begin to recognize our deeper truth: we were never broken, only believing we were.

Today, reflect on a self-judgment you have carried. Can you admit it—without shame, without resistance—simply as it is? In doing so, you create space for healing and release.

I consciously admit my self-judgments,
forgive them, allowing light and truth to dissolve illusion.

Noticing

Noticing is the gateway to presence. When we bring gentle awareness to our thoughts, emotions, and surroundings, we see that life is constantly unfolding in subtle and profound ways. Noticing requires no effort—only openness. It invites us to observe without judgment, to witness without interference, and to simply be with what is.

Today, pause and notice. Notice the breath, the space between thoughts, the sensations in the body. Notice how life continues to move, whether or not you try to control it.

I rest in the simplicity of noticing,
allowing awareness to reveal the richness of each moment.

JUNE 24

DELIGHT

Delight is the natural response to life's mystery, paradox, and wonder. It arises when we stop demanding certainty and instead embrace the unknown with curiosity and playfulness. The beauty of life is not in having all the answers, but in experiencing the depth of the question itself.

Today, find delight in something unexpected. Smile at the absurdity of existence, marvel at life's intricate design, and allow yourself to be enchanted by the mystery.

I delight in the paradox and wonder of life,
embracing its unfolding with joy.

JUNE 25

Knowingness

Knowingness is deeper than belief—it is the direct experience of truth beyond concepts and conditioning. It does not require validation or proof because it arises from the stillness within. When we trust this knowing, we no longer cling to external opinions or mental constructs. We rest in what is.

Today, listen to the knowingness within. Let go of needing to explain or justify it—simply rest in the truth that is already here.

I trust in my knowingness,
allowing truth to reveal itself beyond belief.

JUNE 26

Spaciousness

Beneath every thought, feeling, and experience, there is spaciousness—the vast, open presence of loving awareness. This space is not something to attain; it is already here, underneath all movement and change. When we notice spaciousness, we remember that we are not bound by the passing waves of experience but are the open sky in which they arise.

Today, tune into the spaciousness around and within you. Notice the loving space in and around feelings and sensations; and between breaths. Notice the silence between words, the stillness beneath thoughts and emotions. Rest here.

I rest in spaciousness, allowing all
experience to arise and pass within loving awareness.

JUNE 27

Cheerfulness

Cheerfulness is a lightness of spirit, a way of meeting life with warmth and ease. It does not mean forcing happiness or denying struggle but carrying an openness that allows joy to arise naturally. Cheerfulness is not about circumstances—it is about how we choose to show up for life.

Today, bring cheerfulness into something small. Smile for no reason, share warmth with someone, or find humor in the ordinary. Notice how cheerfulness brightens both your world and the world around you. Get up and do a joy dance waving your arms wildly overhead—that will do it!

I embrace cheerfulness, allowing lightness and
joy to uplift my spirit and those around me.

JUNE 28

Peacefulness

Peacefulness is already here—it is not something we must chase, but something we allow. When we stop struggling against life, peace naturally reveals itself. True peacefulness is not about external circumstances but about resting in the stillness beneath all change.

Today, allow peacefulness to be present. Notice the spaces of quiet between thoughts, the gentle rhythm of the breath, the effortless unfolding of this moment—allowing feelings to be as they are. Peace is always here in the effortless wholeness of experiencing, waiting for you to notice.

I surrender to peacefulness,
allowing the stillness of being to hold experience just as it is.

JUNE 29

Relaxation

Relaxation is a surrender, a softening into the natural flow of life. It is not something to force or achieve—it happens when we release tension, both in the body and in the mind by honestly acknowledging what we may be avoiding. When we let go of resistance to meeting life and experiencing directly with loving curiosity, we find that relaxation is not just physical; it is a state of presence, trust, and ease.

Today, take a moment to relax—not by doing something, but by letting go of the need to hold everything together. Breathe deeply. Allow yourself to rest in the effortless rhythm of being.

I allow relaxation to arise naturally,
releasing all tension into the flow of life.

JUNE 30

Simplicity

Simplicity is clarity. When we strip away the unnecessary—excess thoughts, worries, distractions and false needs and wants we believe sustain us—we find that what remains is already enough. Life is already whole in its simplest form, and when we stop complicating it, we discover a sense of ease and freedom.

Today, simplify something. Whether in your thoughts, actions, surroundings, or material possessions, let go of what is unnecessary and embrace the beauty of less-is-more.

I welcome simplicity, allowing life's natural ease to guide me.

Happiness

Happiness is not something we need to earn—it is our essential nature. It is always available, waiting for us to allow it. When we give ourselves permission to be happy for no reason at all, we free ourselves from the idea that happiness must be justified. True liberation is realizing that happiness can arise in any moment, simply because we choose to welcome it. Because unconditional happiness is our very nature—always present.

Today, allow yourself to be happy—for something, for nothing, for everything. Let go of the idea that happiness must be deserved, earned, qualified, quantified, or justified; and simply let it be.

I allow happiness to arise naturally,
knowing that joy is my essential nature.

Choosing

Life is a series of choices, whether we recognize them or not. Each moment presents us with the power to choose—our mindset, our response, our direction. Even when answers are unclear, the act of choosing moves us forward. Noticing this power brings freedom; accepting it brings responsibility.

Today, be aware of your choices. Even in the smallest things, recognize that you are choosing. And when faced with uncertainty, trust that each choice is a step in your unfolding path.

I embrace the power of choosing, allowing wisdom to guide my path.

JULY 3

Invulnerability

True invulnerability is not about building walls—it is about absolute openness. When we fully embrace our vulnerability, we see that there is nothing to defend, nothing to protect. In surrendering the illusion of control by accepting the okayness of feeling vulnerable, we discover a deeper strength—one that cannot be shaken by fear or resistance.

Today, practice absolute vulnerability. Allow yourself to be open, to be seen, to be without defenses. Notice how, in this openness, you become truly invulnerable.

Through absolute vulnerability,
I reveal my true invulnerability.

JULY 4

Generosity

Generosity is more than giving—it is a state of being. When we give freely, without expectation, unconditionally, we align with the natural abundance of life. True generosity is not just about material things; it includes our time, our attention, and our presence. The more we give from the heart, the more we recognize that generosity itself is its own reward.

Today, offer generosity in a way that feels natural. It could be a kind word, deep listening, or a simple act of care. Notice how giving expands your heart.

I embrace generosity, allowing love
and abundance to flow through me.

Surrendering

Surrendering is not giving up—it is releasing the illusion of control. It is an act of trust, allowing life to unfold without resistance. When we surrender, we are somehow allowing everything to be as it is; especially what the body is feeling, sensing, perceiving. By mercifully opening our hearts and minds to the reality of this moment, there is an unconditional acceptance—surrender. In the grace of surrender, we soften into the natural flow of existence, no longer grasping or forcing. In letting go, we find a deeper peace.

Today, notice where you are holding on too tightly. Can you let go, just a little? Trust that in surrendering, you make space for life's wisdom to move through you.

I surrender to the flow of life, trusting in its unfolding wisdom.

Lovingness

Lovingness is not something to attain—it is our natural essence when fear and resistance are surrendered. It is the effortless warmth of an open heart, a presence that radiates kindness without condition. When we embody the lovingness that we are, we become a channel for love itself, as it flows freely without concern for outcomes; shining its light on all beings beyond judgment.

Today, let lovingness guide your actions. Extend kindness to yourself and others, not because it is deserved or earned, but because it is simply what you are.

I rest in lovingness, allowing love to flow through me without condition.

Kindness

Kindness is a quiet strength, a way of moving through the world with gentleness and care. It requires no grand gesture—sometimes, the smallest acts carry the deepest impact. When we practice kindness, we soften our own hearts and remind others of their own goodness. Kindness is actually a quality, a gift of being human; always here, when we allow its grace to be noticed.

Today, offer kindness in a small, simple way. A kind thought, a kind word, a kind action—each one ripples outward in ways you may never see.

*I choose kindness, knowing that even
the smallest act has the power to uplift.*

Unending

Life has no true beginning or end—only the timeless unfolding of creation. Beneath all change, there is something unchanging, something vast and formless that flows through everything. When we rest in this awareness, we see that we are not separate from life, but part of its infinite unfolding. Amid the constant change of experience there is a loving awareness that witnesses, observes, watches everything. This unending awareness is YOU.

Today, notice the unending nature of life—the breath that continues, the sky that stretches beyond sight, the Loving Awareness that remains through every passing moment. You are not apart from this; you ARE this.

I rest in the unending flow of life, knowing I am creation itSELF.

Fun

Fun is an essential part of life's balance. It reminds us not to take ourselves too seriously, to play, to explore, and to enjoy the absurdity of existence. Fun is not just for children—it is a gateway to joy, creativity, and freedom at any age. When we engage in playfulness, we reconnect with our inner lightness, releasing stress and stepping into the present moment with curiosity and openness. Fun allows us to experience life with fresh eyes, reminding us that joy is not something to be earned, but something to be embraced.

Today, do something for the sheer joy of it. Dance, laugh, be silly—let fun take the lead, without the need for justification. Allow yourself to feel free, even for just a moment.

I welcome fun into my life, allowing joy and
playfulness to uplift my spirit.

Breakdown - Breakthrough

Breaking down IS breaking through. When old patterns crumble, when illusions fall apart, when we feel like everything is unraveling—this is not an ending, but a doorway. In the space where something breaks, something new is born. Every breakdown is an invitation to deeper clarity, transformation, and awakening.

Today, if you find yourself in struggle, pause. Instead of resisting, ask: What is breaking open within me? Trust that in the falling away, something greater is emerging.

I embrace breakdown as breakthrough,
knowing that transformation comes through release.

Presence

When everything else fades—when thoughts quiet, when sensations come and go, when experience rises and dissolves—what remains is presence—pure Loving Awareness. It is not something to create or achieve; it is already here. The silent awareness beneath all movement is reality; please know this. In presence, as presence, as the living awareness that you are, there is nothing to hold onto, yet nothing is missing. Loving Awareness, Presence, is already, always, enough; herenow.

Today, rest in presence. Allow all experiences to come and go, without clinging or resisting. Notice that presence remains, steady and untouched.

I rest in presence, allowing all to arise
and fade within the stillness of being.

Readiness to Feel

Readiness is not about forcing change—it is about allowing it. When we become entirely ready to free ourselves from self-criticism, judgment, blame, guilt, and unworthiness, we do so by turning toward what we have been avoiding. By feeling fully, without resistance, we create space for healing. Readiness is not about being fearless—it is about being willing.

Today, ask yourself: Am I ready to let go? If resistance arises, meet it with kindness. Trust that readiness unfolds naturally when you allow yourself to feel.

I am ready to release self-judgment
by allowing myself to feel fully and freely.

Allowing Calmness

Calmness is not something to chase—it is something we allow. When we stop resisting what is, when we soften into the present moment, calmness naturally arises. It is always here beneath the noise, waiting to be noticed. Like a still lake beneath rippling waves, calmness is never truly absent—we only need to look beyond the surface. The more we allow calmness, the more it becomes our resting place, a steady refuge in the midst of life's uncertainties.

Today, instead of trying to become calm, simply allow it. Take a breath. Notice the space between thoughts. Relax into what already is. Let calmness meet you where you are, and trust that it has always been within you.

I allow calmness to arise naturally,
trusting in the peace that is always here.

Deservingness

You do not have to earn your unconditional worth—you are already and always worthy simply for being alive. Deservingness is not based on accomplishments, perfection, or validation. Or, the temporary identity you believe you are. It is an unshakable truth that whatever you are is are already enough, already loved, already whole. The only step is allowing yourself to receive what has always been yours.

Today, let go of any belief that you must prove yourself. Instead, affirm: I am worthy, simply because I exist.

I allow myself to receive love, joy,
and abundance, knowing that I am inherently deserving.

Meditation

Meditation is not about stopping thoughts—it is about resting in awareness. It is the simple act of being with what is, without resistance. When we meditate, we do not force stillness; we allow ourselves to notice the stillness that has always been here beneath the movement of the mind. In true meditation, we simply do not attach our attention to thoughts, feelings, sensations, or emotions. We simply notice and allow, with loving appreciation and kindness, the unfolding of experience just as it is; as felt in the body-mind.

Today, take a few moments to simply sit. Let thoughts come and go. Feel the breath. Rest in presence. Nothing to do, nothing to achieve—just being.

I allow meditation to be effortless,
resting in the loving awareness that is always here.

Celestial

There is something celestial in all of us—something vast, luminous, and infinite. The same intelligence that moves the stars moves within you. When we connect with this truth, we no longer see ourselves as small or separate, but as part of the great cosmic unfolding.

Today, take a moment to look at the sky, feel the breath of the wind, or simply close your eyes and sense the vastness within. You are not apart from the universe—you are the universe.

I embrace my celestial nature, knowing I am a reflection of the infinite.

Abiding

To abide in love as awareness is to rest in the truth of what we are. Love is not something to chase—it is the ground of being, the very nature of existence. When we abide in this love, we do not grasp, cling, or seek—we simply allow love to be what it is, and let our attention rest in it.

Today, let yourself abide in love. Not love as a feeling or action, but as the unshaken presence that holds all things sacred.

I abide in love as awareness, resting in the peace of my true nature.

Alrighty Then!

Sometimes, life asks for deep reflection. Other times, it just asks for a playful shrug and an "Alrighty then!" Not everything needs to be analyzed, fixed, or figured out. Some moments are meant to be laughed at, embraced, and met with a light heart.

Today, let go of unnecessary overthinking. When life throws something unexpected your way, meet it with ease. Smile, breathe, and say, "Alrighty then!"

I allow life to unfold as it is, meeting each moment with trust and ease.

Timelessness

Beyond the ticking of clocks, beyond the stories of past and future, there is only this—the eternal now. Timelessness is not found in escaping time but in realizing that presence has never left. When we stop measuring life by moments gained or lost, we discover that we have always been here.

Today, notice timelessness. Feel the breath. Watch a leaf move in the wind. Rest in the space where time dissolves, and only presence remains. The loving awareness that you infinitely are.

I embrace the timeless nature of being, resting in the eternal now.

JULY 20

Energy

Energy flows where attention goes. Whether subtle or powerful, it moves through every thought, word, and action. When we become aware of energy, we realize we are not separate from it—we are it. Balanced, focused energy fuels clarity, joy, and well-being.

Today, notice your energy. Where is it flowing? Is it scattered or focused? Honor it. Nurture it. Let it move with intention.

I align with the natural flow of energy,
allowing it to guide and uplift me.

JULY 21

Eating Consciously

Eating is more than fueling the body—it is an act of connection, gratitude, and presence. When we eat consciously, we honor where our food comes from, how it nourishes us, and the life energy it carries. Awareness transforms eating from a routine habit into a sacred practice.

Today, eat with mindfulness. Notice the colors, textures, and flavors. Chew slowly. Appreciate the nourishment. Let eating be a moment of stillness and gratitude.

I eat with awareness, honoring my
body and the nourishment life provides.

JULY 22

Natural Self-Worth

Your worth is not something you need to prove, earn, or justify—it is already yours. It is untouched by past mistakes, external opinions, or fleeting successes. Your innocence, your worth, your deservingness have always been here, simply because you exist.

Today, affirm your natural self-worth. Stand in it. Breathe it in. Know that nothing can take it away.

I am innocent. I am worthy. I am deserving—just as I am.

JULY 23

Life

Life is not a problem to solve, nor a journey to complete—it is simply happening, here and now. It moves through us, around us, and as us. When we stop trying to control it and instead allow ourselves to be it, life unfolds effortlessly, as it always has.

Today, let life be. Observe, feel, and participate, without grasping or resisting. Simply allow.

I surrender to life, trusting in its natural unfolding.

Self-Inquiry

Self-inquiry is not about judgment—it is about understanding. When we turn inward with humility and compassion, we begin to see that our beliefs, behaviors, feelings, and even our suffering arise from innocent misunderstanding. Through meditative self-inquiry, we observe without resistance, allowing truth to reveal itself naturally.

Today, pause and look within. Gently ask: What am I believing right now? Is it true? Meet whatever arises with kindness, knowing that self-inquiry is not about fixing but about seeing clearly.

I turn inward with compassionate curiosity,
allowing truth to reveal itself.

Effortlessness

Life flows effortlessly, like a gentle river freely flowing without a care in the world, when we stop resisting it. Effortlessness is not about avoiding action but about allowing things to unfold naturally, without struggle, without allowing the obsessive mind to dictate and control our attention. When we release the need to force, push, or control, we discover that presence itself carries us and our attention naturally rests in the peaceful heart of grace. Just as the breath moves without effort, so too does life when we trust its rhythm.

Today, notice where you are forcing or striving. Can you soften, even slightly? Let go and allow life to move through you, effortlessly.

I trust in the natural flow of life,
allowing effortlessness to guide me.

Truthfulness

Truthfulness is not just about speaking honestly—it is about living in alignment with what is real. It requires the compassionate courage to see our experience clearly, without illusion or pretense. It is about allowing ourselves to tenderly acknowledge what we have been avoiding and choosing acceptance instead. When we are truthful, we no longer need to hide behind masks or stories of untruths and denial. Truth liberates, dissolving the weight of falsehood and bringing clarity to our lives. Allowing the loving presence that we are shine through.

Today, practice truthfulness—not just in words, but in presence. Where can you let go of pretending? Where can you meet life as it is?

I embrace truthfulness, allowing clarity
and authenticity to guide my way.

Space

Space is the vast cosmic presence that allows all things to arise. Without space, the elements could not move, form, or create. It is the infinite backdrop upon which existence unfolds, the silent openness that holds both galaxies and the smallest breath. This space is not separate from us—it is what we are.

Today, notice the space around you, the stillness between sounds, the openness beneath all experience. You are not just what moves within space—you are space itself.

I rest in the infinite space of being,
allowing all things to arise and dissolve within me.

Freedom

True freedom is not about escaping—it is about recognizing that nothing has ever truly bound us. The mind may tell stories of limitation, but beneath them, we are already free. Freedom is the ability to meet life fully, to befriend experience without resistance or fear. It is the choice to surrender control and trust the flow of existence.

Today, notice where you feel restricted. Is the limitation real, or is it only a belief? Release the need to be free, and simply realize— you already are.

I embrace the truth of my freedom,
knowing that nothing can confine my being.

Sincerity

Sincerity is the art of showing up fully, without pretense. It is speaking from the heart, listening with presence, and acting in alignment with our truest intentions. A sincere life is one of openness, trust, and deep connection—both with ourselves and with others. When we live sincerely, we let go of masks and false appearances, embracing authenticity instead. Sincerity does not mean perfection; it means honesty, vulnerability, and the willingness to engage with life as it truly is. It creates deeper relationships, fosters understanding, and invites others to meet us in the same genuine space.

Today, bring sincerity into your interactions. Speak honestly, listen deeply, and let your actions reflect your truth.

I move through life with sincerity,
honoring the depth and authenticity of my being.

Liberty

Liberty is more than external freedom—it is the inner state of being unbound. It is the realization that no thought, belief, or past experience can truly confine us unless we allow it to. When we embrace liberty, we see that we are not victims of circumstance but creators of our experience.

Today, reflect on where you are holding yourself captive. What happens when you release the illusion of limitation? Step into the liberty that has always been yours.

I embrace my inner liberty, knowing I am free in every moment.

Collective Well-Being

We are not separate from the whole—what we think, say, and do ripples outward, shaping the world around us. Our inner peace contributes to outer peace. Our kindness uplifts not just one, but many. When we recognize that our well-being is intertwined with all of existence, we begin to move through life with greater care, responsibility, and love.

Today, notice how your thoughts, words, and actions affect the collective. Choose to contribute to well-being—both yours and the world's.

I honor the truth that my presence affects
the whole, and I choose to nurture collective well-being.

AUGUST 1

Glory

Glory is not about recognition or achievement—it is the radiant unfolding of life itself. It shines in the rising sun, in the quiet strength of presence, in the limitless potential within each moment. True glory is not something to attain; it is something to witness, to embody, to allow.

Today, pause and recognize the glory of existence. See it in the simplest things—in breath, in movement, in the light of awareness itself.

I embrace the glory of life,
knowing it is ever-present within and around me.

AUGUST 2

Life is a Mirror

Life reflects back to us exactly what we need to see. Every joy, every struggle, every relationship serves as a mirror, revealing our inner world. When we embrace this, we stop seeing life as something happening to us and begin to recognize it as a reflection of our own awareness, inviting us to grow and awaken.

Today, observe life as a mirror. What do your experiences reveal? Instead of resisting, allow yourself to learn from what is being reflected back to you.

I see life as a mirror, allowing its
reflections to guide my growth and awakening.

Liberation

L iberation is not something given to us—it is realized. It is the recognition that we were never truly bound, only believing we were. The moment we stop identifying with the fears, judgments, and limitations of the mind, we see that we have always been free. Liberation is not about escape—it is about awakening to what has always been. It is the release of self-imposed barriers, the surrender of conditioned stories, and the deep knowing that nothing outside of us can imprison our spirit. True liberation is a shift in perception, an opening to the vastness of existence beyond mental constructs.

Today, reflect on what you believe is holding you back. Is it real, or is it a story? What happens when you let go of the belief in limitation?

I embrace liberation, knowing that I am already free.

Wholeness

W holeness is not something to be attained—it is already here. Beneath every perceived flaw, beyond every story of lack, you are whole. Nothing needs to be added or fixed. When we stop searching outside ourselves and turn inward, we remember that we have never been broken. Wholeness is our natural state, always present, even when we forget or doubt it.

Today, rest in your wholeness. Let go of striving. Let go of the idea that something is missing. Simply be.

I embrace my wholeness,
knowing that I am complete just as I am.

AUGUST 5

Worthiness

Worthiness is not something we earn—it is inherent, natural, already an essential ingredient of our being. No mistake, no past action, no external judgment can take away your essential worth. The fact that you are alive gives you infinite worthiness and unconditional value. The only step is recognizing it. When we fully accept our worthiness, we stop seeking validation in all the wrong places and allow ourselves to receive the love, joy, and peace that have always been ours—already within.

Today, affirm your worth by feeling it. Notice any thought that tells you otherwise, and gently let it go. You are already enough.

I honor my natural worthiness,
allowing myself to receive all that life offers.

AUGUST 6

Expressiveness

Expressiveness is the freedom to allow what is within us to flow outward. It is the courage to speak, create, and move in ways that reflect our truth. When we suppress expression, we limit our natural energy. When we embrace it, we align with the authentic unfolding of our being.

Today, express yourself freely. Speak from the heart, create without fear, move without hesitation. Let yourself be seen. Remember, you are an expression of life, allowed and free to be as you are.

I embrace my natural expressiveness,
allowing my truth to flow without restriction.

AUGUST 7

Universe

The universe is not something outside of us—it is what we are.
Every breath, every thought, every moment is the universe
unfolding as you. When we stop seeing ourselves as separate,
we recognize that we are part of something infinite, vast, and
interconnected.

Today, take a moment to feel your connection to the universe.
Look at the sky, feel the ground beneath you, sense the life moving
through you. You are not in the universe—you are the universe.

I am the universe in motion, inseparable from all that is.

AUGUST 8

Expansiveness

There are no real limits to what you are. Expansiveness is the
natural state of being—wide, open, and boundless. The mind
creates walls, but awareness has no edges. When we stop contracting
into fear, we experience the vastness of our true nature.

Today, notice expansiveness. Feel the open sky, the depth of
breath, the stillness between thoughts. Let go of constriction and
allow yourself to expand into the infinite.

I rest in expansiveness, knowing that I am limitless awareness.

AUGUST 9

Making Amends

True healing begins with honesty. When we acknowledge those we
believe we have harmed, we open the door to reconciliation—

not just with others, but within ourselves. Becoming willing to make amends is an act of courage, humility, and love. It is not about guilt or self-punishment, but about restoring harmony where disharmony once existed.

Today, reflect on those you may have affected with your words or actions. Can you hold them in your heart with sincerity and a willingness to heal? Even before taking action, willingness itself is a powerful step.

I open my heart to making amends,
allowing healing and reconciliation to unfold.

AUGUST 10

Reverence

Reverence is a deep respect for life itself. It is seeing the sacred in the ordinary, honoring each breath, each moment, each being as an expression of the divine. When we move through life with reverence, we no longer take things for granted—we recognize the miracle in everything.

Today, practice reverence. Whether in silence, in nature, or in a simple interaction, let yourself honor what is before you.

I move with reverence, honoring the sacredness in all things.

AUGUST 11

Befriending Feelings and Emotions

For much of our lives, we have been conditioned to resist our feelings—pushing away sadness, suppressing anger, avoiding discomfort. We judge emotions as if they are enemies, labeling them as "good" or "bad," "acceptable" or "unacceptable." But emotions are not mistakes. They are not intrusions. They are simply experiences passing through us, asking to be seen, felt, and acknowledged.

When we stop fighting our emotions, when we let go of fighting what we are feeling, experiencing, we create space for healing. Instead of resisting, we can learn to sit with feelings and sensations, to befriend them, to listen to what they are telling us. Every emotion has a purpose—whether it's grief calling us to slow down, anger pointing us toward our boundaries, or joy reminding us of our capacity for love.

Today, instead of pushing a feeling away, try welcoming it. Say to yourself: I see you. You are allowed to be here. Notice what happens when you stop resisting and start embracing.

I befriend my emotions, allowing all feelings
to arise and move through me with kindness and presence.

AUGUST 12

Companionship

Though our journey is uniquely our own, we do not walk it without friends. In the wildly amusing mystery of existence, no one can do it for you, yet you cannot do it alone. Companionship reminds us of our shared humanity, the warmth of connection, and the beauty of witnessing and being witnessed. Whether in deep friendship or a fleeting smile from a stranger, we are all walking each other home.

Today, appreciate the companions on your journey. Acknowledge those who have supported you, and offer your presence to another.

I cherish the companionship of others,
knowing we are all connected in this journey.

Sacred Listening

To truly listen is to be fully present. Sacred listening is more than hearing words—it is receiving another's truth without interruption or judgment. It is also listening inwardly, hearing the quiet wisdom within. In this space of deep listening, connection and understanding emerge.

Today, practice sacred listening. Whether with another person, in nature, or in meditation, listen deeply, without the need to respond or fix—just receive.

I offer sacred listening, allowing
presence to deepen connection and understanding.

Welcoming Change

Change is not the enemy; it is the essence of life. When we resist change, we suffer. When we welcome it, we open ourselves to growth, renewal, and new possibilities. Every transformation, even the difficult ones, carries the seed of something greater. Change invites us to shed what no longer serves us, to evolve beyond limitations, and to step into new versions of ourselves. When we trust in the unfolding of life, we see that change is not happening to us but for us, guiding us toward deeper wisdom and expansion.

Today, instead of resisting change, welcome it. Ask: What is life inviting me into? Trust that even in uncertainty, something meaningful is unfolding. What new possibilities are waiting to emerge?

I welcome change, knowing that
transformation leads to growth and renewal.

AUGUST 15

Unfolding

A flower does not rush its bloom, nor does it force itself to open before its time. Life unfolds in its own rhythm, and so do we. When we stop forcing and allow ourselves to unfold naturally, we align with the deeper intelligence of existence.

Today, let go of the need to control your process. Trust that you are unfolding exactly as you need to.

I trust in the natural unfolding of my life,
knowing that everything blooms in its own time.

AUGUST 16

Beyond Fear

Fear is not the enemy—it is a doorway. When we meet fear with awareness, we see that it is not something to eliminate, but something to move through. Beyond fear lies freedom, clarity, and the realization that we were never truly trapped—only believing we were.

Today, observe any fears that arise. Instead of pushing them away, acknowledge them. Ask: What happens if I move through this fear instead of resisting it?

I move beyond fear, trusting that freedom lies on the other side.

AUGUST 17

Receiving

It is often easier to give than to receive. Yet, receiving is just as important—it allows us to accept love, support, and abundance without resistance. To receive fully, we must let go of unworthiness and the need to always be in control. True receiving is an act of trust.

Today, allow yourself to receive. Whether it is a kind word, help from another, or the simple beauty of the present moment, open your heart and accept it fully.

I welcome the gifts of life with an open heart,
allowing myself to receive freely.

AUGUST 18

Deep Rest

Deep rest is more than sleep—it is the stillness that comes when we stop striving, stop clenching, stop trying to hold everything together. It is surrendering into the present moment, trusting that we do not need to be in control. When we allow ourselves to truly rest, healing happens naturally.

Today, give yourself permission to rest—not just physically, but mentally and emotionally. Let go of the need to accomplish, and simply be.

I allow myself deep rest, knowing that
life supports me even when I pause.

AUGUST 19

The Quiet Center

Amidst the noise of thoughts, emotions, and the world around us, there is a quiet center within. It is always there, unshaken, unaffected, holding the stillness of presence. When we remember this center, we are no longer tossed around by life—we find peace in the middle of everything.

Today, take a moment to rest in your quiet center, allowing your kind attention to rest in the heart of loving awareness. Close your eyes, take a breath, and feel the stillness that has always been here.

I return to my quiet center, knowing that peace is always within me.

Radiance

You do not have to become radiant—you already are. The mind may cloud over this light with doubt and self-judgment, but the radiance of your being has never dimmed. When we stop hiding, stop shrinking, and stop holding back, we allow our true essence to shine effortlessly.

Today, let your radiance be seen. Smile, express, move through the world without fear of your own light.

I embrace my natural radiance, allowing my inner light to shine freely.

Wholeheartedness

To live wholeheartedly is to show up fully—to bring our absolute attention to each moment, unguarded and open. It requires courage, vulnerability, and a willingness to embrace life with sincerity. When we engage wholeheartedly, we stop holding back and experience life more deeply.

Today, practice wholeheartedness. Be fully present in whatever you do—whether speaking, listening, creating, or simply being.

I embrace life wholeheartedly,
allowing my presence to be full and open.

Soft Strength

Strength is often mistaken for hardness, but true strength is soft. It does not resist—it flows. It does not dominate—it allows. The strongest trees bend with the wind, the deepest rivers carve mountains with gentle persistence. Soft strength moves as trust rather than force.

Today, embrace the power of softness. Instead of resisting, allow. Instead of pushing, flow. Strength is not in control, but in trust.

I embrace soft strength, allowing life to move through me with grace.

The Art of Letting It Be

Not everything needs to be fixed, changed, or controlled. Sometimes, the most powerful action is to let things be. When we stop grasping, stop resisting, stop forcing, we make space for peace. Letting it be does not mean passivity—it means trusting life's unfolding without unnecessary interference.

Today, practice letting it be. Notice where you are trying to force an outcome, and see what happens when you release the need to control.

I trust in the art of letting it be, allowing life to unfold as it will.

Mindfulness

Mindfulness is the practice of being fully aware—of our thoughts, words, and actions as they arise. It is the ability to notice unnecessary inner dialogue and judgmental thoughts before they take hold, as well as to observe how we express ourselves outwardly. True mindfulness is not about perfection but about presence—the willingness to see clearly and to take responsibility when needed.

Today, stay mindful of your inner and outer world. Notice thoughts before they become words, and words before they become actions. And if harm is caused, admit it promptly, allowing mindfulness to guide you back to balance.

I remain mindful and alert, allowing loving awareness
to shape my thoughts, words, and actions with care.

AUGUST 25

Resilience

Resilience is not about never falling—it is about rising again, each time with deeper wisdom. Life's challenges are not meant to break us but to reveal the strength we already carry. True resilience comes not from resisting difficulties, but from moving through them with awareness and grace.

Today, reflect on your own resilience. Where have you risen before? Trust that whatever arises, you have the capacity to meet it.

I embrace resilience, knowing that
every challenge is an opportunity for growth.

AUGUST 26

Simplicity in Being

Life is naturally simple—it is the mind that complicates it. We clutter our thoughts with unnecessary worries, our actions with endless striving, and our hearts with imagined burdens. When we strip away the excess, what remains is pure being—free, present, and whole.

Today, practice simplicity. Let go of what is unnecessary. Rest in the quiet truth that you are enough, just as you are.

I embrace simplicity in being,
allowing myself to exist without strain or effort.

AUGUST 27

Compassion for the Self

We are often our own harshest critics, holding ourselves to impossible standards while offering kindness freely to others. Yet, we are just as deserving of compassion. When we meet ourselves with gentleness, we soften the edges of self-judgment and open to healing.

Today, speak to yourself with the same kindness you would offer a friend. If self-criticism arises, pause and replace it with compassionate understanding.

I offer myself compassionate understanding,
knowing that I am worthy of kindness and care.

AUGUST 28

Interconnectedness

Nothing exists in isolation. Every breath we take is shared with the world, every action ripples outward, every being is woven into the vast web of existence. When we recognize our interconnectedness, we move with greater care, knowing that what we do for another, we also do for ourselves.

Today, notice the ways you are connected—to people, to nature, to life itself. See how even the smallest actions contribute to the whole.

I honor my interconnectedness,
knowing that all beings are reflections of the same essence.

Authentic Speech

Words hold power—they can heal or harm, uplift or divide. Authentic speech arises when we speak with truth, kindness, and awareness of impact. It is not about saying what is expected, but about honoring both honesty and compassion in communication.

Today, be mindful of your words. Before speaking, ask: Is it true? Is it kind? Is it necessary? Let your words be a reflection of your deepest integrity.

I choose authentic speech,
speaking with honesty, kindness, and awareness.

Non-Attachment

Attachment creates suffering when we cling to things, people, or outcomes as if they define us. Non-attachment does not mean not caring—it means engaging with life fully while releasing the need to control. When we let go, we discover freedom in the flow of existence.

Today, practice non-attachment. Notice where you are holding on too tightly—whether to a thought, a feeling, or an expectation. Breathe, soften, and let it be.

I embrace non-attachment,
trusting that life unfolds as it is meant to.

AUGUST 31

Unraveling

Not all growth is about building—sometimes, it is about unraveling. Old beliefs, outdated patterns, and unhelpful fears loosen and dissolve when we stop holding onto them so tightly. In unraveling, we make space for something truer to emerge.

Today, notice what is unraveling within you. Instead of resisting, allow it. Trust that whatever is falling away is making room for something new.

I trust the process of unraveling,
allowing what no longer serves me to dissolve.

SEPTEMBER 1

Gracious Receiving

Just as giving is an act of love, so is receiving. Many of us resist accepting kindness, feeling unworthy or uncomfortable. But when we receive with openness, we acknowledge our interconnectedness—we allow others to give, and we affirm that we, too, are deserving.

Today, practice gracious receiving. Accept a compliment, a kind gesture, or support without hesitation. Allow yourself to receive with gratitude, knowing that giving and receiving are one.

I receive with an open heart,
knowing that I am worthy of life's gifts.

SEPTEMBER 2

The Wisdom of Pausing

Between impulse and action, between thought and speech, there is a sacred space—the pause. In this space, we find clarity, wisdom, and the ability to choose with awareness. Pausing is not inaction; it is the moment where true presence begins.

Today, practice pausing. Before reacting, before deciding, take a breath. Notice how this simple act creates space for a wiser response.

I honor the wisdom of pausing,
allowing presence to guide my actions.

Seeing Beyond Appearances

We often judge things by their surface—the way a person looks, the way a situation appears, the way we feel in a single moment. But deeper truth is rarely found in appearances. When we look beyond the mind's surface judgments and reactive opinions, we see things as they truly are—without illusion, without assumption. We become aware of the natural beauty in everyone, everything.

Today, practice looking deeper. Before judging, pause. Before assuming, inquire. Let yourself see beyond appearances, and witness the essence beneath.

I see beyond appearances,
allowing deeper truth to reveal itself.

Centering Prayer

Centering prayer is the practice of consenting to divine action within us. It is not about asking, striving, or seeking—it is about surrendering. By choosing a sacred word that symbolizes our willingness to be guided, we quiet the mind and open our hearts to the presence already here.

Today, choose a word that reflects your deepest surrender—peace, love, trust, or whatever speaks to you. Let it be your anchor, returning to it throughout the day as a silent meditation of acceptance.

I consent to divine action,
allowing grace to move through me in stillness and trust.

Innate Value

You were born with infinite, unconditional value. Nothing can add to it, and nothing can take it away. The mind may believe worth must be earned, that you must be a specific way and live up to societal and familial standards to have worth, but true value is not measured by accomplishments, status, or approval—it simply is. Every being is inherently whole, worthy, and deserving of love.

Today, rest in your innate value. Let go of striving for worthiness and recognize that you already are enough, exactly as you are.

I embrace my innate and natural value,
knowing I am whole, worthy, and complete just as I am.

The Heart Knows

The mind analyzes, questions, and doubts, but the heart knows. Beneath the noise of overthinking, there is a deeper wisdom—a quiet, steady presence that does not need logic to guide it. When we trust the heart's knowing, we move through life with clarity and peace. Again, the mind believes but the heart knows beyond belief.

Today, listen to the wisdom of your heart. When faced with a choice, pause and feel into it. Trust what arises in the stillness beyond and prior to thought or thinking.

I trust the knowing of my heart,
allowing its wisdom to guide my path.

Detaching with Love

Letting go does not mean we stop caring—it means we stop trying to control. Detaching with love allows us to release expectations, attachments, and the need to change others. Rumi said, "Allowing someone to have the experience they are having is the greatest act of love." It is an act of trust, knowing that love remains even when we step back from trying to impose our egoic-will on another.

Today, practice detaching with love. Where can you loosen your grip and trust the process? Breathe, release, and know that love is not about control—it is in allowing.

I detach with love,
trusting that all unfolds as it is meant to.

Loving Kindness

Loving kindness is an active practice of holding others—friends, family, strangers, even those we struggle with—in the warmth of our hearts. When we consciously send love to all beings, we soften resentment, expand compassion, and connect to the infinite love that flows through everything.

Today, take a moment to close your eyes and bring someone to mind. Whisper, "May you be happy. May you be at peace. May you be free from suffering." Extend this kindness to yourself, and then to the world.

I cultivate loving kindness,
holding all beings in love and compassion.

Liberation from Suffering

Suffering arises not from life itself, but from the mind's resistance to it. An unenlightened mind clings to illusions, rejects what is, and remains trapped in stories of past and future. But freedom from suffering is possible—not by changing life, but by changing our relationship to it. When we meet each moment with awareness and surrender, suffering dissolves, revealing the peace that has always been here.

Today, notice where suffering arises. Is it from life itself, or from resistance to life? What happens when you simply allow things to be as they are?

I embrace liberation from suffering,
knowing that peace is found in accepting what is.

Right View

Clarity begins with seeing things as they truly are. The Four Noble Truths teach that suffering exists, has a cause, can end, and that there is a path to liberation. When we recognize this, we stop running from discomfort and start meeting life with understanding. Right View is not just intellectual—it is a shift in how we perceive reality.

Today, reflect on how you view suffering. Do you resist it, or do you see it as a doorway to deeper understanding?

I cultivate Right View,
seeing life with clarity and wisdom.

Right Intention

Our intentions shape our lives. Right Intention means letting go of greed, hatred, and delusion while nurturing thoughts of loving-kindness, compassion, and non-harm. When our intentions are clear and wholesome, our actions naturally align with wisdom and peace.

Today, pause before acting or speaking. Ask yourself: Is this coming from love or fear? Choose intention over impulse.

I cultivate Right Intention,
aligning my thoughts with kindness and clarity.

Right Speech

Words can heal or harm, connect or divide. Right Speech is speaking truthfully, kindly, and with purpose—avoiding gossip, harshness, and falsehoods. Our words shape not only our relationships but our inner world.

Today, practice mindful speech. Before speaking, ask: Is this true? Is it kind? Is it necessary? Notice how conscious speech brings peace.

I practice Right Speech, using my words to uplift and bring clarity.

Right Action

Our actions ripple outward, affecting ourselves and others. Right Action means living ethically—refraining from harm, dishonesty, and exploitation. When we act with integrity, we create harmony within and around us.

Today, be mindful of your actions, even in small ways. Ask: Does this align with my highest values? Choose actions that reflect your deepest truth.

I cultivate Right Action,
moving through the world with integrity and care.

SEPTEMBER 14

Right Livelihood

Right Livelihood is earning a living in a way that supports, rather than harms, life. It is not just about work—it is about the energy we bring into the world. When our livelihood aligns with ethics, we contribute to the well-being of all.

Today, reflect on how your work and actions impact others. Whether in your job or daily interactions, choose to engage in a way that uplifts rather than harms.

I cultivate Right Livelihood,
ensuring that my work aligns with truth and compassion.

SEPTEMBER 15

Right Effort

Growth requires effort—but not struggle. Right Effort is about actively cultivating positive qualities while releasing harmful habits. It is the balance between discipline (not punishment) and allowing, persistence and patience.

Today, put effort into something that brings wisdom or peace. Whether through meditation, kindness, or releasing a negative pattern, take one step forward. Give yourself permission to listen to the deepest loving intelligence within; and let it guide you.

I cultivate Right Effort, directing my energy
toward what nourishes and uplifts.

SEPTEMBER 16

Right Mindfulness

Right Mindfulness is the practice of being fully present, without judgment or distraction. It is seeing thoughts, emotions, and sensations clearly—without getting lost in them. When we live mindfully, life becomes richer, and we respond rather than react.

Today, practice mindfulness in one simple act—eating, walking, listening. Be fully present. Notice the difference when you give your full awareness.

I cultivate Right Mindfulness,
embracing each moment with presence and clarity.

SEPTEMBER 17

Right Concentration

A scattered mind is restless; a focused mind is peaceful. Right Concentration is the practice of steadying the mind through meditation, allowing us to see the nature of the mind while noticing and observing reality with clarity and depth. When the mind is calm, insight arises naturally. When the mind is noisy, we simply watch without attaching our attention to the mental commentary.

Today, take a few moments to focus on your breath. Each time the mind wanders, gently bring it back. Notice how with earnest practice to direct your attention, by focusing it where you choose, concentration is enhanced.

I cultivate Right Concentration,
allowing clarity and insight to deepen within me.

SEPTEMBER 18

It's Okay to Make Mistakes

Mistakes are not failures—they are teachers. Every misstep, every moment of imperfection, is an opportunity to learn, grow, and deepen in awareness. When we release self-judgment and embrace mistakes as part of the journey, we move with more ease, curiosity, and openness.

Today, if you make a mistake, meet it with kindness instead of criticism. Ask: What can I learn from this? Let mistakes be stepping stones, not obstacles.

I allow myself to make mistakes,
knowing that growth comes through learning.

SEPTEMBER 19

Nature Immersion

Nature is not separate from us—it is a reflection of what we are. When we immerse ourselves in the natural world, we reconnect with something grounding and deeply healing; an ever-present lifeforce. The stillness of a forest, the rhythm of the ocean, the vastness of the sky—each moment in nature reminds us to slow down, breathe, and simply be.

Today, take time to step outside, even for a few moments. Feel the breeze, listen to the sounds around you, notice the life unfolding effortlessly. Let nature remind you of your own natural rhythm.

I immerse myself in nature,
allowing its presence to ground and restore me.

Patience with the Process

Everything in nature unfolds in its own time. Flowers do not rush to bloom, rivers do not force their flow, and the sky does not hurry the rising sun. Growth, healing, and awakening follow the same rhythm. When we force, we create tension. When we trust, we allow life to unfold as it is meant to.

Today, practice patience with yourself and your process. Notice where you are trying to rush an outcome. Instead, breathe and trust—everything is unfolding as it should.

I trust in the process,
knowing that growth happens in its own perfect timing.

The Beauty of Slowness

In a world that glorifies speed, slowness is a forgotten art. When we slow down, we become aware of life's richness—the feel of the breath, the warmth of the sun, the depth in a single moment. Slowness is not stagnation; it is presence. It allows us to experience life fully rather than rushing past it.

Today, slow down. Walk a little more gently, eat a little more mindfully, listen with full presence. Notice how life opens when you give it space.

I embrace the beauty of slowness,
allowing presence to deepen my experience of life.

Deep Listening

True listening is more than hearing—it is presence. It is quieting the mind, releasing the urge to respond, and fully receiving what is being shared. When we listen deeply, we create space for understanding, connection, and healing. This applies not only to others but also to ourselves—listening to the whispers of our own heart.

Today, practice deep listening. In conversation, let go of preparing a response and simply be with the other person. In solitude, turn inward and listen to what arises without judgment.

I cultivate deep listening,
allowing space for connection and truth to emerge.

The Pathless Path

There is no singular way to awakening, no fixed map to inner peace. The journey is unique for each of us, unfolding moment by moment. When we stop looking for a set destination and instead embrace the present, we realize that the path has been beneath our feet all along.

Today, let go of the need to know exactly where you are going.

Walk the pathless path—trusting that each step reveals itself exactly when it needs to.

I release the search for a fixed path
and trust in the unfolding journey of life.

Seek to Understand

So often, we listen to respond rather than to understand. We seek to be heard, to be validated, to be right. But true connection arises when we shift our focus—not to being understood, but to understanding. When we approach others with curiosity instead of judgment, we open the door to deeper compassion and insight.

Today, practice seeking to understand. In conversation, listen with presence. Ask questions. Let go of the need to prove a point. Notice how understanding deepens when you make space for it.

I seek to understand, knowing that true connection arises from deep
listening and open-hearted presence.

Beyond the Idea of Wrongdoing

Rumi wrote, "Beyond the ideas of wrongdoing and right-doing, there is a field. I will meet you there." Beyond judgment, beyond blame, beyond the mind's need to divide things into good and bad, there is only love. Unconditional love does not ask who is right or wrong—it simply embraces what is. When we step beyond judgment, we enter a space of deep understanding, peace, and connection.

Today, practice moving beyond the idea of wrongdoing and

right-doing. Pause and ask: "What happens if I meet this moment with love instead of judgement?"

I step beyond judgment, resting in
the unconditional love that embraces all things.

Attending to the Body

The body holds everything—tension, stress, unspoken emotions, and past experiences. When we bring loving attention to it, we allow healing to unfold. Attending to the body is not about fixing but about listening, about offering kindness to the places that need it most.

Today, take a moment to check in with your body. Where do you feel tension, tightness, or unease? Breathe into that space with love, offering gentle attention without judgment. Let your body know it is safe to release.

I attend to my body with kindness,
allowing love and awareness to bring healing where it is needed.

Feeling Fully

Emotions are meant to be felt, not suppressed or avoided. When we allow ourselves to experience them fully—without resistance or judgment—we give them space to move through rather than get stuck in the body experience. Feeling fully is not about losing control but about meeting emotions with openness and curiosity.

Today, when an emotion arises, let it be. Instead of pushing it .

away or analyzing it, simply feel it. Notice where it lives in your body, breathe into it, and allow it to move naturally.

I allow myself to feel fully,
trusting that every emotion has its place and purpose.

Emotions as Messengers

Every emotion carries a message. Anger may reveal boundaries that need strengthening. Sadness may point to something we need to release. Fear may be asking for deeper trust. When we listen to our emotions rather than dismiss them, they become guides rather than burdens.

Today, pay attention to what your emotions are telling you. Instead of reacting, ask: What is this feeling trying to show me? Welcome its wisdom.

I listen to my emotions with curiosity,
allowing them to guide me toward greater self-awareness.

The Wisdom of Tears

Tears are not a sign of weakness—they are a release, a cleansing, a natural response to deep feeling. Whether from joy, sadness, grief, or relief, crying is the body's way of processing and letting go. There is wisdom in allowing ourselves to soften, to surrender, to feel without shame.

Today, if tears arise, let them come without resistance. Allow them to flow freely, knowing they are part of your healing. Tears are not weakness; they are a release, a cleansing of unattended sorrow, a deep expression of what is asking for loving attention, within.

I honor my tears as a natural expression of emotion,
allowing them to cleanse and renew.

SEPTEMBER 30

Sitting with Discomfort

Difficult emotions are not meant to be avoided—they are meant to be met with presence. When we sit with discomfort instead of running from it, we build resilience, self-awareness, and inner peace. The more we allow ourselves to be with what is, the less power it has over us.

Today, if discomfort arises, pause. Instead of distracting yourself, sit with it. Breathe into it. Notice how, when given space, even the most difficult emotions soften.

I sit with discomfort, knowing that
presence dissolves resistance and brings clarity.

Embracing Joy Without Fear

Joy is often accompanied by a quiet fear—the fear that it won't last. We hesitate to embrace happiness fully, bracing ourselves for disappointment. But joy is not something to protect ourselves from—it is something to surrender into. The more we allow joy, the more deeply it fills us. Joy is not fragile; it does not need to be controlled or rationed. It exists in the present moment, independent of past losses or future uncertainties. When we stop guarding against it, we realize that joy is not fleeting—it is always available, waiting to be welcomed fully.

Today, let joy in without hesitation. Bask in its warmth, knowing you are worthy of its presence, no matter what tomorrow may bring. Let yourself feel it completely. Don't shrink away or question it—simply receive it.

I allow myself to embrace joy fully,
knowing that happiness is meant to be felt, not feared.

The Space Between Emotion and Reaction

Between the rise of an emotion and the action that follows, there is a space. In that space lies the power to choose. Reacting impulsively often leads to regret, but when we pause, we give ourselves the opportunity to respond with wisdom, grace, and conscious clarity.

Today, practice pausing. When an emotion arises, take a breath before acting. Notice how even a brief moment of awareness can change the course of your response.

I create space between my emotions and my actions,
allowing awareness to guide me.

OCTOBER 3

Releasing Emotional Baggage

We carry emotions longer than we need to—grief that has settled in the body, resentment that tightens the heart, guilt that weighs on the soul. But we are not meant to hold onto every feeling forever. When we release emotional baggage, we free ourselves to live more fully in the present.

Today, reflect on what emotional weight you may still be carrying. Ask yourself: Is this still serving me? If not, breathe deeply and begin the process of letting go.

I release what no longer serves me,
allowing space for renewal and peace.

OCTOBER 4

Loving the Parts of Ourselves We Hide

We all have emotions and traits we try to suppress—anger, insecurity, sadness, fear. Yet, these parts of us need love, not rejection. When we embrace the aspects of ourselves we've hidden, we integrate them into wholeness rather than allowing them to fester in the shadows.

Today, bring kindness to a part of yourself you have judged or ignored. Instead of pushing it away, meet it with love.

I welcome all parts of myself with compassion,
knowing that I am whole just as I am.

The Breath and Emotion Connection

Our breath is the bridge between body and mind. When emotions run high, breath becomes shallow and rapid. When we consciously breathe, we soothe the nervous system, creating space for awareness and calm. Learning to use the breath allows us to regulate emotions rather than be ruled by them.

Today, notice your breath when emotions arise. If tension builds, take slow, deep breaths. Allow the breath to carry you back to balance.

I use my breath to regulate emotions,
finding ease and presence in every inhale and exhale.

Honoring the Inner Child

Deep within us lives the child we once were—the part of us that still holds old fears, unmet needs, and long-forgotten joys. Honoring the inner child means offering them the love, safety, and reassurance they may not have received. It is a way of healing the past while nurturing the present.

Today, take a moment to connect with your inner child. What does that part of you need? Speak to them kindly, as you would a small child who simply wants to feel loved.

I honor my inner child with love and care,
offering them the safety and kindness they deserve.

OCTOBER 7

Totality

Life is whole, even when it appears fragmented. Every moment, every experience, every breath is part of the totality of existence. When we stop dividing life into good and bad, right and wrong, we begin to see that everything is included—nothing is outside of this wholeness.

Today, embrace the totality of your experience. Instead of rejecting parts of life, welcome them. See how everything belongs.

I trust in the totality of existence,
knowing that nothing is separate from the whole.

OCTOBER 8

Impermanence

Nothing stays the same. Every feeling, thought, and experience arises, lingers for a time, and then fades. When we grasp at permanence, we suffer. Freedom comes in knowing that everything passes, and that is okay.

Today, notice impermanence in small ways—a breath coming and going, a moment of tension dissolving, a leaf drifting to the ground. Let this truth bring peace rather than fear.

I embrace impermanence, knowing that change is the nature of all things.

Emptiness

Emptiness is not nothingness—it is vast possibility. When we let go of rigid identities, fixed beliefs, and attachments, we create space for something new. Emptiness is openness, a freedom from limitation. In seeing that nothing has a fixed, permanent self, we realize that everything is interconnected and flowing. At a deeply profound level the Buddha was once asked, "Who are you?" and his response was, "Emptiness."

Today, soften your grip on who you think you are or how life should be. Notice how spaciousness arises when you stop holding on so tightly to self-images and self-concepts.

I embrace emptiness as openness,
allowing life to unfold without attachment.

Nothingness

Nothingness is not the absence of life—it is the infinite space in which everything arises. Just as the sky holds the clouds without being the clouds, nothingness is the foundation of all existence. When we release the innocent need to fill every moment with thought and distraction, we discover the peace and grace of simply being.

Today, take a moment to rest in nothingness. Not a concept of nothingness, but nothingness as unconditional loving presence. Close your eyes, breathe, and let yourself experience the stillness beneath all movement—pure being.

I rest in the nothingness that holds all things,
knowing that presence requires nothing at all.

Completeness

Y ou are already whole. There is nothing missing, nothing broken, nothing to be found outside of yourself. The mind may tell stories of lack, but at your core, you are already complete. When we stop searching and simply allow ourselves to be, we realize that everything we need is already here. We recognize that who we temporarily and innocently believe ourselves to be was born whole, worthy, complete; still is; and always will be. This completeness, wholeness, enoughness, is the underlying reality of yourSELF.

Today, affirm your completeness—the pure loving reality that you are; that no one can take away; not even your mind. Release the belief that something outside of you will make you whole. You already are, prior to believing and identifying as anything.

I embrace my completeness,
knowing that I lack nothing in this moment.

Changing

N othing remains the same—not the body, not the mind, not the world around us. Change is constant, whether we welcome it or resist it. When we flow with change instead of fearing it, we move with grace rather than struggle.

Today, reflect on something that has changed in your life. Instead of mourning what was, celebrate what is. See how each change has brought you to where you are now.

I embrace change as a natural part of life,
knowing that transformation is always unfolding.

Universality

At the deepest level, we are not separate. Separation is merely a concept innocently invented by the mind. Of course, every expression of the universe is unique, but NOT separate. We are made of the same elements, breathe the same air, and share the same fundamental desires for love, peace, and understanding. Every life-form and creation of existence, both intangible and tangible, arise from the same source. Universality reminds us that beyond and prior to surface differences and physical appearances, we are one.

Today, look beyond labels and divisions. Perceive before the mind distorts pure perception. See the shared essence in every being you encounter. Recognize yourself in others.

I embrace universality, knowing that
all beings are interconnected in the fabric of existence.

Selflessness

Selflessness is not the loss of identity—it is the freedom from the illusion of separateness. When we let go of the idea that we are separate from others, we move with greater compassion, generosity, and presence. In selflessness, we find true fulfillment—not by taking, but by giving.

Today, practice selflessness in a small way. Offer kindness, patience, or a moment of presence to another without seeking anything in return.

I release the illusion of separateness,
knowing that true fulfillment comes through selfless presence.

Forgiveness

Forgiveness is not about excusing harm—it is about freeing ourselves from the weight of resentment, hate, and self-judgment. Holding onto anger and other afflictive emotions keeps us bound to the past, while forgiveness allows us to move forward with peace. True forgiveness is not a mental act, but a deeper allowing, to free ourselves from burdens that no longer serve us. It is a gift we give to ourselves, a release that opens space for healing, clarity, and renewal. When we forgive, we reclaim our energy, choosing love and freedom over bitterness and pain.

Today, reflect on what you are ready to release. Bring to mind something you have been holding onto. Can you soften, even just a little? Let go, not for the other person, but for yourself. What would it feel like to let go and step into peace?

I choose forgiveness, knowing that letting go brings freedom and peace.

Love

Love is not just an emotion—it is the essence of existence. It is the undercurrent of all things, the invisible force that binds us together. Love does not need to be earned or deserved—it simply is. When we stop searching for love outside of ourselves and realize it is already within us, we move through the world differently.

Today, allow love to flow freely—from yourself, to yourself, and through yourself. Love needs no reason.

I rest in the presence of love,
knowing that it is my natural state of being.

Maturity

Maturity is not about age—it is about awareness. It is the ability to see beyond immediate reactions, to respond with wisdom rather than impulse. Maturity is also about self-honesty, genuinely admitting there are feelings or situations that may need your loving attention. Meeting life with presence, understanding that not everything needs a reaction, and that patience often brings the deepest clarity, are profound realizations arising from maturity.

Today, practice maturity by pausing before reacting. Take a deep breath before acting out of blame, judgment, or fear. Choose compassionate understanding over frustration, wisdom over anger, presence over reactivity.

I cultivate maturity by responding
to life with wisdom and presence.

Integrity

Integrity is the alignment of thoughts, words, and actions. It is living in a way that reflects our values, even when no one is watching. When we act with integrity, we build trust within ourselves and with others. It is not about being perfect—it is about being honest, aware, and true to what we know is right.

Today, reflect on where you can bring greater integrity into your life. Speak with honesty, act with kindness, and move in alignment with your highest truth.

I embody integrity, aligning my thoughts,
words, and actions with truth and sincerity.

OCTOBER 19

The Mirror of Relationship

Every relationship is a mirror, reflecting back to us the parts of ourselves that need attention, healing, or growth. When we feel triggered by another, it is often because something within us is asking to be seen. Likewise, the love and kindness we receive are reflections of what already exists within us.

Today, notice how your relationships act as mirrors. Instead of reacting, ask: What is this showing me about myself?

I embrace relationships as reflections,
allowing them to guide my growth and understanding.

OCTOBER 20

Giving and Receiving Love

Love flows freely when we allow both giving and receiving. Many of us feel comfortable giving but struggle to receive—rejecting compliments, pushing away help, or feeling unworthy. But love is not meant to be one-sided; it is a balance, an open exchange of energy.

Today, practice receiving love as openly as you give it. When someone offers kindness, let it in.

I allow love to flow freely, giving and receiving with an open heart.

OCTOBER 21

Healthy Boundaries

Boundaries are not barriers; they are bridges to deeper connection. When we set healthy boundaries, we honor both ourselves and others. Without them, resentment builds, and relationships suffer. True boundaries are rooted in self-respect, not fear.

Today, check in with your boundaries. Are there places where you need to say no? Or places where you can soften?

I honor my needs and set boundaries with clarity, love, and self-respect.

The Art of Deep Presence

In a world of distractions, presence is one of the greatest gifts we can offer. True connection happens not through words alone, but through being fully with another—seeing, listening, and holding space without needing to fix or change anything.

Today, practice deep presence. In conversation, put down your phone, quiet your mind, and truly listen. Notice how connection deepens when you give your full attention.

I offer my full presence, knowing
that true connection begins with being fully here.

Letting Go of Expectations

We often place expectations on others—how they should act, respond, or love us. Of course, we do this to ourselves all of the time. When someone does not meet those expectations, we feel hurt in the same way when we naively believe we haven't lived up to our personal expectations; then often judge ourselves. But love is not about controlling another or holding ourselves to unattainable standards; it is about accepting ourselves and others as we are. It is about feeling what we are feeling right now, without believing it should be a different way. Letting go of expectations allows us to experience the loving felt-sense of life more freely and empowers relationships to unfold naturally.

Today, notice where you are holding expectations in relationships. Can you release them and meet others as they are?

I let go of expectations, allowing love to flow freely and authentically.

The Power of Vulnerability

True connection is built in moments of vulnerability—the willingness to be seen, to share our fears, joys, and struggles without hiding. When we let go of the need to appear perfect, we create space for genuine love and understanding.

Today, take a step toward vulnerability. Share something real with someone you trust, or simply allow yourself to feel without judgment.

I embrace vulnerability,
knowing that it is the foundation of true connection.

OCTOBER 25

Appreciating the People in Our Lives

Love thrives in appreciation. Too often, we take those closest to us for granted, assuming they know how much they mean to us. But love deepens when expressed—through words, actions, and presence.

Today, take a moment to appreciate someone in your life. Send a message, offer a kind word, or simply hold them in gratitude.

When we open our minds and hearts to cultivating the most sacred qualities of being human, like loving appreciation, we naturally feel lighter, freer.

I cherish the people in my life,
expressing appreciation with an open heart.

OCTOBER 26

Healing Through Relationship

Relationships reveal our wounds, but they also hold the power to heal them. When old fears, insecurities, or patterns arise in connection with others, they are invitations to heal—not by blaming, but by bringing awareness and love to what surfaces.

Today, if a relationship stirs something difficult within you, pause. Instead of reacting, ask: What is this teaching me about myself?

I embrace relationships as spaces for healing,
allowing love to transform old wounds.

OCTOBER 27

When to Hold On, When to Let Go

Not all relationships are meant to last forever. Some grow with us, while others come to teach, challenge, or guide us for a time before fading. Knowing when to hold on and when to let go is an act of wisdom, trust, and love.

Today, reflect on a relationship in your life. Is it nourishing or depleting? Growing or stagnant? Allow yourself to release what no longer serves with grace and gratitude.

I trust the natural flow of relationships,
holding on when appropriate and letting go with peace.

Love as a Daily Practice

Love is not just something we feel—it may be something we consciously bring our attention to, daily, in our words, actions, and presence. It is in small gestures, quiet understanding, and the way we choose to show up for one another. Love is not an abstract idea—it is alive in every moment we choose to embody it. In fact, love is the essence of what we are. Our true nature is unconditional love. Let love radiate without concern for results. Let it flow, effortlessly.

Today, let love be your effortless practice. Offer kindness without reason, listen with an open heart, and meet others with warmth and without expectations or trying to get something in return.

I choose love as a daily practice,
allowing it to guide my words, actions, and presence.

Understanding Feelings

Feelings are more than emotions—they are sensations in the body, often attached to stories. A racing heart may be labeled as anxiety, a warm chest as love, a tight stomach as fear. But when we strip away the mental narratives, we see feelings for what they truly are—temporary experiences moving through us.

Today, when a strong feeling arises, pause. Instead of attaching a story, simply notice the sensations. What happens when you feel without judgment?

I observe my feelings as passing sensations,
allowing them to arise and fade without attachment.

It's Okay to Have Feelings

Feelings are natural. They do not make us weak, wrong, or unworthy. They are simply part of being human. Yet, we often judge ourselves for feeling too much, too deeply, or at the "wrong" times. But emotions are not mistakes—they are signals, guiding us toward understanding and healing.

Today, remind yourself: It's okay to feel. Whatever arises, allow it without resistance. Meet your emotions with kindness, as you would a dear friend.

I honor my feelings, knowing they are a
natural and valid part of my experience.

Acknowledging Resistance

Resistance often arises when life does not match the stories we have told ourselves about how things should be. We may hold onto expectations, struggling against reality instead of flowing with it. But resistance itself is not the problem—it is the invitation. When we acknowledge it, we open the door to awareness and change.

Today, notice where resistance shows up. Instead of fighting it, simply acknowledge it. Ask: What story am I holding onto? Let awareness create space for something new.

I acknowledge my resistance with curiosity,
allowing life to unfold as it is.

Making Space for Healing

Healing does not happen when we are rushed, distracted, or overwhelmed. It happens when we create space—when we slow down, breathe, and allow ourselves to be with whatever is asking for our attention. Healing is not about forcing or fixing; it is about softening and allowing.

Today, make space for healing. Take a deep breath. Release the urgency to be "better" or "fixed." Simply allow yourself to be where you are, with kindness.

I create space for healing, allowing it to unfold in its own time.

The Gift of Uncertainty

We often fear uncertainty, believing we must have all the answers. But uncertainty is not the enemy—it is the space where possibility lives. When we stop resisting the unknown, we open ourselves to discovery, growth, and new paths we never could have planned.

Today, instead of fearing uncertainty, welcome it. Ask: What if this unknown is leading me somewhere beautiful? Give uncertainty and not knowing a change and see what the mystery of life has been offering here all along.

I embrace uncertainty as a doorway to new possibilities.

Learning to Trust Again

When trust is broken—by others, by life, or even by ourselves—it can feel safer to close off. But healing requires reopening. Trust is not about guarantees; it is about choosing to soften despite the past. It is about believing that life still holds goodness, that love is still possible, and that we are strong enough to take the risk.

Today, take one small step toward trust. Even if it's just trusting yourself to keep showing up.

I allow trust to grow,
knowing that healing happens one step at a time.

Inner Strength vs. Control

We often mistake control for strength. But true strength does not come from grasping, forcing, or trying to manage every outcome. It comes from trust. It comes from surrendering to life as it is, while knowing that we can meet whatever arises with resilience and grace.

Today, notice where you are trying to control. What happens when you release your grip?

I embrace inner strength, trusting in life rather than controlling it.

Softening into Presence

Tension, stress, and worry are signs that we are resisting the present moment. Softening into presence means allowing ourselves to be here—without clenching, without pushing, without trying to escape. Presence is always available when we allow our attention to relax into it.

Today, notice where tension lives in your body. Breathe into it. Soften. Let yourself arrive in this moment fully.

I soften into presence,
allowing attention to rest in the here and now.

NOVEMBER 6

Honesty with Ourselves

It can be difficult to face certain truths—about our fears, our patterns, or the ways we've avoided healing. But honesty with ourselves is the first step toward real transformation. When we meet our own truth with kindness rather than judgment, we create space for growth.

Today, be honest with yourself. What truth have you been avoiding? Instead of resisting it, meet it with love.

I embrace honesty with myself,
knowing that truth leads to freedom.

NOVEMBER 7

Being Open to Being Wrong

The need to be right often keeps us stuck. Growth happens when we release our attachment to always having the answers and instead remain open to learning. Being wrong is not failure—it is an opportunity to see more clearly, to expand our perspective, to grow in wisdom.

Today, practice openness. If you feel defensive, pause and ask: What if there's something I haven't yet seen?

I release the need to be right and
remain open to greater understanding.

Grieving What Never Was

Not all grief comes from losing something we had—sometimes, it comes from losing something we hoped for. Dreams unfulfilled, paths not taken, love that never arrived. Acknowledging these quiet losses allows us to release them and move forward with peace.

Today, honor what never was. Give yourself permission to grieve, knowing that letting go makes space for new beginnings.

I allow myself to grieve what never was,
trusting that life continues to unfold in beautiful ways.

Walking Away with Grace

Letting go is not always easy, but sometimes it is necessary. Whether it is a relationship, a belief, or a situation that no longer serves us, walking away does not have to be an act of anger—it can be an act of love. Graceful endings allow us to move forward with peace.

Today, reflect on something you may need to release. Can you let go with gratitude, rather than resistance?

I walk away with grace,
trusting that every ending is also a beginning.

Nothing is Missing

The mind often tells us that we are lacking—lacking love, success, purpose, or wholeness. But beneath these thoughts, there is a deeper truth: nothing is missing. We are already complete. What we seek is not outside of us, but within.

Today, rest in the knowing that you are already enough. You do not need to be more, do more, or have more. You are whole, herenow.

I embrace the truth that nothing is missing; I am already whole.

Sun

The sun shines without effort, without hesitation, without waiting for permission. It gives warmth, light, and life to all things, asking for nothing in return. Even on cloudy days, its presence remains, steady and unwavering. Like the sun, we too have an inner light—one that is always present, even when obscured by passing storms.

Today, take a moment to feel the warmth of your own inner radiance. You do not need to force it—simply allow it to shine naturally, just as the sun does.

I embrace my inner light, shining freely without hesitation or expectation.

Rivers and Streams

Rivers and streams do not resist—they move with ease, carving paths through mountains, nourishing the land, and finding their way to the vast ocean. They do not cling to one place, nor do they fear change. Their strength lies in their ability to flow.

We, too, are meant to move with life rather than resist it. When we let go of rigid expectations and trust the current, we find that life carries us exactly where we need to go.

Today, reflect on where you might be resisting life's natural flow. What happens when you soften and trust the movement?

I flow like a river, trusting that life's
currents will guide me where I need to be.

Birds Singing

Birds do not wait for the perfect conditions to sing—they sing because it is their nature. They do not question whether their song is worthy, nor do they seek permission. Their voices rise with the dawn, filling the world with music simply because they are alive.

We, too, have a voice, a presence, a song to share. We do not need to wait for the "right" moment to express ourselves, to bring joy, to embrace life. The beauty of our existence is reason enough.

Today, let yourself sing—whether in words, laughter, kindness, or presence. Let yourself express freely, without hesitation.

I embrace my voice and presence,
sharing my song with the world in my own way.

Wildlife

Wildlife moves with an effortless grace, untouched by the burdens of overthinking or self-doubt. A deer does not question its worth. A wolf does not hesitate in its howl. A butterfly does not seek approval before unfolding its wings. In nature, every being exists in its purest, most unencumbered state—fully alive, fully present.

We, too, are part of this wild, sacred existence. Beneath the noise of the mind, there is something natural within us—something free, instinctual, and whole.

Today, take a moment to appreciate the raw, unfiltered essence of life around you. Can you allow yourself to move through the day with the same effortless presence?

I honor the wildness within and around me,
embracing life in its natural, unencumbered glory.

NOVEMBER 15

Oceans and Seas

The ocean is the great mother, the original incubator of life. Its waves have carried the rhythms of existence long before we arrived, and its waters remain within us—more than 70% of our bodies are saltwater, mirroring the vastness from which all life emerged.

Like the sea, we are deep, fluid, and ever-changing. Beneath the surface of thoughts and emotions, there is a stillness, a depth that cannot be disturbed. When we return to this awareness, we remember that we are not separate from the ocean—we are the ocean, moving through life with a timeless, boundless presence, loving awareness, infinite grace.

Today, close your eyes and imagine the sea within you. Feel its vastness, its movement, its power. Trust that, like the ocean, you are deep, strong, and ever-flowing.

I embrace the depth and fluidity within me,
knowing I am part of the vast ocean of life.

The Wisdom of the Moon

The moon does not fight its cycles—it waxes and wanes, knowing that each phase is necessary. It does not resist the darkness of the new moon or cling to the brightness of the full moon. It simply follows its rhythm, trusting in the ebb and flow of change. Trusting in the impermanence of experience.

We, too, go through cycles—times of fullness and times of retreat, times of clarity and times of uncertainty. The wisdom of the moon reminds us that each phase is sacred, and nothing is ever truly lost.

Today, honor the phase you are in. Trust that, like the moon, you are always in the right part of your journey.

I embrace the natural cycles of my life,
knowing that each phase carries its own wisdom.

Breathing with the Earth

The earth breathes with us. With each inhale, trees and plants offer oxygen; with each exhale, we return carbon dioxide to fuel new life. This cycle of breath is a reminder that we are deeply connected to all things—our very existence is intertwined with the earth's rhythms.

Today, take a moment to breathe with awareness. Feel the breath as an exchange with nature, a loving union and communion with the world around you. With each inhale, receive life. With each exhale, perfect giving.

I breathe with the earth, feeling my deep connection to all of existence.

Forgiving Feelings and Emotions

Many of us carry silent guilt for simply feeling what we feel. We may believe we *shouldn't* be sad, *shouldn't* be angry, *shouldn't* be overwhelmed. But this resistance—this self-judgment—creates more suffering. Without realizing it, we make an enemy of our own emotions, pushing them away rather than embracing them as part of our human experience.

Forgiveness is a powerful act of healing. To forgive our feelings is to free ourselves from the inner war against what naturally arises. Instead of resisting, we can soften. Instead of rejecting, we can welcome. When we say, *I forgive you. You are allowed to be here,* we offer ourselves the compassion we have been withholding.

Today, take your attention directly to a feeling or sensation in your body. Instead of judging it, speak to it kindly: *I forgive you. You are welcome here.* Notice how this simple act of forgiveness creates space for healing.

I forgive my feelings and emotions, allowing
them to be exactly as they are, without resistance or shame.

The Dance of Opposites

Life moves in opposites—light and dark, expansion and contraction, joy and sorrow. One cannot exist without the other. Just as the night makes the sunrise more beautiful, challenges make peace more meaningful. The dance of opposites is not a battle—it is balance. It is the duality of experience designed perfectly to provide context and content to our lives. This divine place of experience in the dance of opposites arises from the unchanging reality that we are—pure infinite loving awareness. Remember, you are not the body and not even the mind.

Today, if you find yourself in a difficult moment, remember that it is part of a greater rhythm that comes and goes. The tide will shift, as it always does.

I embrace the dance of opposites,
knowing that balance arises from all experiences.

NOVEMBER 20

Mountains and Strength

Mountains do not rush, nor do they bend to the wind. They stand in quiet strength, not through force, but through presence. They remind us that true strength is not about control, but about being deeply rooted in humility, unshaken by passing storms.

Today, embody the strength of a mountain. Stand graciously in your truth, knowing that real power comes from quiet steadiness, compassionate understanding, and grace, not from resistance.

I embrace the steady strength within me,
rooted and unshaken like the mountains.

NOVEMBER 21

The Gift of Surrender

Surrender is not about giving up—it is about releasing the need to control everything. It is an opening, a softening, a deep trust in life's unfolding. When we stop resisting, we allow grace to enter.

Today, notice where you are holding on too tightly. What happens if you surrender, even just a little? Let go and trust that life is carrying you.

I surrender to the flow of life, knowing that trust brings peace.

NOVEMBER 22

The Beauty of the Ordinary

Life is not just made up of big moments—it is woven together by the simple, ordinary ones. The warmth of the sun on your skin. The sound of laughter. The rhythm of breath. When we stop chasing what's extraordinary, we see that the sacred is everywhere.

Today, find beauty in something small. Pause. Notice. Appreciate.

I find beauty in the ordinary,
knowing that life's magic is always present.

NOVEMBER 23

Cycles of Renewal

Nature teaches us that endings are never truly endings—every falling leaf makes way for new growth, every tide that recedes will return. We, too, experience cycles of renewal. What feels like loss is often the beginning of something new.

Today, reflect on what is ending in your life. Instead of mourning the change, welcome the space it creates for new possibilities.

I trust in the cycles of renewal,
knowing that every ending brings a new beginning.

The Heart's Compass

The mind seeks logic, but the heart knows the way. The heart's compass does not need proof or certainty—it simply senses truth. When we learn to listen, to trust its quiet pull, we find ourselves moving toward what is most authentic and aligned.

The heart speaks in subtle ways—a feeling of expansion, a sense of ease, a quiet knowing that transcends words. It does not argue or analyze; it simply offers guidance, waiting for us to notice. When we tune in, we begin to navigate life with more trust, intuition, and inner peace.

Today, place your hand over your heart. Breathe. Ask yourself: What is my heart guiding me toward? Listen.

I trust the wisdom of my heart,
allowing it to guide me with clarity and love.

Living as the Sky

The sky does not hold onto passing clouds. It does not resist storms or cling to sunshine—it simply allows all things to come and go, knowing that its vastness remains untouched. We, too, can live this way—allowing emotions, experiences, and thoughts to move through us, without becoming them.

Today, practice being like the sky. Notice thoughts, feelings, and events as passing clouds. Let them come and go, while remaining steady in your vast awareness.

I live as the sky, open and vast,
allowing all things to pass through me without resistance.

NOVEMBER 26

Life is Process in Motion

Life is not a fixed destination—it is a continuous unfolding, a process in motion. Like a river that never stops flowing, life is always shifting, evolving, and transforming. When we try to hold onto moments, identities, or outcomes too tightly, we create resistance. But when we embrace life as a process, we move with ease, trusting that each step leads naturally to the next.

Today, notice where you are trying to control life's flow. What happens when you allow things to be in motion, without grasping or resisting?

I embrace life as a process in motion,
trusting its natural unfolding.

NOVEMBER 27

Flourish

To flourish is to grow abundantly—not just to survive, but to thrive in mind, body, and spirit. Flourishing does not mean perfection; it means embracing growth, opening to new experiences, and allowing life to flow through us without resistance. Like a tree expanding toward the sky, flourishing happens when we nurture our inner world with care, presence, and love. When we open our hearts and minds to infinite possibility—we are free.

Today, open your heart and mind to infinite possibility. And take a few moments to lovingly reflect on what helps you flourish. What environments, thoughts, and actions support your well-being?

I allow myself to flourish,
trusting in my natural ability to grow and expand.

Thrive

Thriving is not about external success—it is about being fully alive. It is the ability to grow through challenges, to move with resilience, and to embrace joy without fear. Thriving does not mean we never struggle, but that we continue to choose life, presence, and possibility.

Today, notice where you are simply getting by and ask yourself: What would help me thrive instead? Even the smallest shift can create momentum.

I choose to thrive, embracing life
with energy, resilience, and gratitude.

Growth

Growth is not always comfortable. It stretches us, challenges us, and asks us to step beyond what is familiar. But every experience—whether joyful or painful—carries the potential for expansion. True growth comes when we stop resisting change and instead welcome it as part of life's unfolding. And at a visceral level, the felt sense of life, inner growth and healing flourishes when we allow ourselves to feel whatever we have been avoiding.

Today, reflect on how you've grown over time. What lessons have shaped you? What challenges have strengthened you? What feelings are you hiding from? Honor the process.

I embrace growth, knowing that every experience deepens my
understanding and awareness.

Optimism

Optimism is not about ignoring difficulties—it is about choosing to see possibilities beyond them. It is the willingness to believe in light even in dark moments, to trust that challenges will pass, and to keep moving forward with an open mind and heart.

Today, practice optimism. When doubt arises, ask: What else might be possible here? Notice how shifting your focus shifts your energy.

I choose optimism, knowing that life holds
infinite possibilities beyond what I can see.

DECEMBER 1

Empowerment

Empowerment is the recognition that we are not victims of life—we are active participants. It is the realization that we have the ability to shape our experiences, to choose our perspectives, and to step into our full strength. When we reclaim our power, we stop waiting for life to change and begin creating from within.

Today, ask yourself: Where am I giving my power away? Shift your focus toward what you can do, and take one confident yet gentle step in that direction.

I stand in my power,
knowing that I am capable, strong, and free.

DECEMBER 2

Enthusiasm

Enthusiasm is the spark of life—a natural excitement that arises when we are fully engaged in what we love. It is a reminder that joy is not something we must seek; it is something we can bring to every moment. When we cultivate enthusiasm, we transform even the simplest experiences into something meaningful.

Today, approach life with enthusiasm. Find joy in small things, in the beauty of the present moment. Let your energy uplift you and those around you.

I embrace enthusiasm, allowing my joy
and passion to shine through everything I do.

Believe

Belief is a powerful force—it can limit us, or it can set us free. When used wisely, belief helps reorient our attention toward deeper knowing. Instead of clinging to limiting beliefs, we can choose to believe in possibility, in love, in the truth beyond thought. Eventually, belief leads us to something greater—direct experience, where belief is no longer needed.

Today, examine your beliefs. Are they helping or hindering you? What happens if you shift your attention beyond the limitations of belief and toward trust and knowing?

I choose beliefs that guide me toward
truth, presence, and deep inner knowing.

Hope

Hope is a bridge between despair and clarity. It is not the final destination, but a tool—a temporary light to guide us when we cannot yet see fully. Hope helps us move forward when the path is unclear, keeping us afloat until we can return to the deep presence and peace that exist beyond all doubt.

Today, if you find yourself in struggle, allow hope to hold you. Let it lift your gaze toward possibility until your heart remembers this truth beyond fear—that hope is not something we hold onto for our entire lives. It is something we outgrow.

I use hope as a temporary stepping stone,
trusting that I am always being guided toward peace and love.

Freedom from Self-Hate

Self-hate is a heavy burden, one we were never meant to carry. It disguises itself as truth, whispering stories of unworthiness, guilt, and shame. But these voices are not reality—they are learned patterns, echoes of past conditioning. True freedom comes when we release self-punishment, self-condemnation, and the belief that we are inherently flawed.

You do not need to be harder on yourself to be worthy. You do not need to suffer to be deserving of love. Freedom begins when you choose kindness—when you offer yourself the same understanding you would give to your beloved.

Today, take a deep breath and release any lingering self-judgment. You are not your past, your mistakes, or the stories in your mind. You are something deeper—something already whole, already free.

I release self-hate, choosing love, compassion, and freedom instead.

The Strength in Softness

True strength is not about force—it is about resilience, openness, and the willingness to remain soft even in the face of challenges. Water carves through mountains not by resistance, but by flowing effortlessly around obstacles. Softness is not weakness; it is the ability to stay present and open no matter what life brings.

Today, notice where you can bring more softness into your life. Can you meet a difficult moment with gentleness instead of resistance?

I embrace the strength in softness, knowing that
flexibility and openness allow me to move through life with ease.

Being at Home Within Yourself

No matter where we go, the one place we will always inhabit is yourSELF. When we cultivate inner peace by opening our minds and hearts to allowing life to live through us rather than obsessively trying to make life happen the way the mind wants, we carry that sense of home with us wherever we are. Because wherever we are is always Here. Being at home within what appears as a body is greatly about accepting your experience fully; allowing whatever feelings, sensations, thoughts, and perceptions to be as they are without fighting them. When we allow our experience to be as it is, we begin feeling safe in your own presence, and trusting a deeper wisdom.

Today, take a moment to be with yourSELF—not as a critic, but as a loving presence that befriends feelings and whatever is happening.

I am at home within myself,
trusting that I am enough exactly as I am.

Letting Experience Be Enough

We often chase the next goal, the next validation, the next thing we think will make us feel whole. But life is happening now. Every experience, no matter how small, is already complete in itself. When we let go of the need for more, we find joy in simply being.

Today, let whatever you do be enough. Whether big or small, let the experience itself be complete without seeking something more.

I allow each moment to be enough,
trusting that life is already whole as it is.

Acknowledging Instinct

Instincts are powerful forces within us—automatic, embodied responses designed to ensure the survival of the physical body. They urge us to fight, flee, freeze, fawn, protect, eat, and procreate. These impulses arise not from deep spiritual wisdom, but from the evolutionary conditioning of the nervous system. While natural and necessary for navigating the physical world, they do not define who we truly are.

Acknowledging instincts is not the same as identifying with them. We can honor their presence without confusing them for truth or guidance. Instincts are not our essence—they are part of the animal body we inhabit, not the deeper awareness that observes. The spiritual path invites us to evolve beyond automatic reactivity and into conscious choice, responding from presence rather than reflex.

Today, notice when instinctual reactions arise. Instead of blindly following them, pause. Ask yourself: Is this response serving my deeper truth?

I acknowledge my instincts as natural,
yet choose to respond from deeper awareness and understanding.

Releasing Regret

Regret is the weight of the past pressing against the present. But no matter how much we wish something had been different, we cannot change it—we can only change how we carry it. Releasing regret does not mean forgetting; it means learning, forgiving, and allowing ourselves to move forward.

Today, reflect on a regret you have been holding onto. Can you shift your focus from what was to what is possible now?

I release regret, knowing that each moment offers me a new beginning.

DECEMBER 11

Celebrating Small Wins

We often wait for major achievements before celebrating ourselves. But real progress is made in small steps, in quiet moments of growth, in the things no one else sees. When we learn to acknowledge and celebrate these, we cultivate a deep sense of fulfillment.

Today, take a moment to celebrate yourself. Acknowledge something, no matter how small, and let yourself feel proud.

I celebrate every step of my journey,
knowing that growth happens in small, meaningful ways.

DECEMBER 12

Moving with Life, Not Against It

Resistance creates suffering. When we fight what is, we exhaust ourselves in an unwinnable battle. But when we move with life instead of against it—trusting its rhythm, surrendering to its flow—we find a deep and natural ease.

Today, notice where you are resisting life. What happens when you soften, allowing things to unfold instead of forcing them?

I move with life's natural flow,
trusting that everything unfolds in its own time.

Trusting the Unknown

We are often afraid of what we cannot see, but uncertainty is not something to fear—it is the space where possibility lives. When we stop needing all the answers, we open ourselves to unexpected beauty, growth, and transformation.

Today, practice trusting the unknown. Instead of filling the gap with worry, invite kind and tender curiosity.

I trust in the unknown,
knowing that life is always guiding me toward what I need.

The Healing Power of Laughter

Laughter is medicine for the soul. It dissolves tension, brings light to heavy moments, and connects us to joy. Even in difficult times, laughter reminds us that not everything needs to be taken so seriously. Not laughter as a coping skill, but laughter as grace.

Today, find something that makes you laugh. Allow yourself to feel lightness, even for a moment.

I welcome laughter into my life,
knowing that joy is a form of healing.

Your Breath as a Constant Companion

No matter where you are or what is happening, your breath is with you. It is a quiet, steady presence—always available to bring you back to the moment. When the mind races or emotions rise, the breath is a simple, grounding anchor.

Today, take a few deep, mindful breaths. Feel the air move in and out, bringing calm and clarity.

I return to my breath, trusting it as a
steady companion through all of life's moments.

DECEMBER 16

Welcoming Rest Without Guilt

Rest is not laziness. It is not something we must earn. Rest is essential—a time for the body, mind, and spirit to restore, reset, and renew. When we allow ourselves to rest without guilt, we honor the natural cycles of energy and stillness that keep us balanced.

Today, give yourself permission to rest. Let go of the feeling that you must be constantly productive. Simply allow yourself to be.

I welcome rest without guilt,
knowing that renewal is a necessary part of life.

DECEMBER 17

Releasing the Weight of Judgment

Judgment—whether toward ourselves or others—is a heavy burden to carry. It creates separation, fuels resentment, and limits our ability to see with clarity. When we release judgment, we make space for understanding, compassion, and deeper connection. Often, out of our awareness, we are judging the feelings of the body and constantly trying to make them go away or avoid unattended sorrow. We even push our natural sense of joy and happiness away as if they are somehow wrong or we don't deserve to be happy.

Today, notice when judgment arises. Ask, "What feeling am I judging." Instead of clinging to judgment as a coping mechanism, take a deep breath and let it go. See what happens when you meet your feelings and others with openness and loving acceptance instead.

I release judgment, choosing to see and feel with kindness,
compassionate understanding, and clarity.

DECEMBER 18

Awareness Before Action

Not every thought needs a reaction. Not every feeling needs to be acted upon. When we pause before responding, we create space for awareness, allowing us to move with intention rather than impulse. Actually, action does not need thought at all; it can arise on its own from a deeper place of Universal Intelligence, the truth of what we are.

Today, practice pausing. Before speaking, before reacting, before making a decision—take a breath. Notice how awareness creates clarity and that action can arise on its own without force. Just notice.

I choose awareness before action,
allowing presence to guide my responses.

DECEMBER 19

Living with an Open Heart

An open heart is not guarded—it is courageous. For it knows that nothing real can be threatened. It is choosing to love, to connect, to trust, even when the mind wants to build walls. When we live with an open heart, we invite life in fully, embracing both its beauty and its lessons.

Today, soften. Let yourself love freely, without fear. Open your heart, and let life in. In your lived experience, what feels more free, light, and loving: Living from the Heart - OR - the obsessive mind and compulsive reactions?

I live with an open heart,
allowing love and connection to guide my path.

DECEMBER 20

You Are Not Your Thoughts

Thoughts come and go like clouds in the sky. Some are helpful, some are not. But none of them define who we truly are. When we learn to observe our thoughts instead of identifying with them, we find a deep and steady peace beneath the mental noise.

Today, watch your thoughts with curiosity. Instead of believing them, simply notice them—like passing clouds.

I am not my thoughts; I am the awareness that observes them.

DECEMBER 21

Returning to the Present Moment

The mind constantly pulls attention into the past or pushes it into a fictional mental future. But life is always happening now. When we kindly allow attention to return to the present moment, we reconnect with reality, finding peace in what is, rather than what was or could be.

Today, bring your attention to the present. Feel your breath, listen to the sounds around you, and fully arrive in this moment.

I return attention to the present, knowing that life
is only ever happening right now.

The Beauty of Solitude

Solitude is not loneliness—it is the space where we meet ourselves deeply. When we allow ourselves time alone, without distraction, we reconnect with our own presence, intuition, and inner wisdom. Solitude is a gift, offering clarity, insight, and renewal.

Today, take a moment to be with yourself, in stillness. Notice the richness of simply being.

I honor the beauty of solitude,
knowing that within stillness, I find myself.

Creating Inner Stillness

Stillness is not about stopping the world around us—it is about cultivating peace within us. Even in the busiest moments, there is a quiet space inside that remains untouched. When we connect with it, we find calmness, no matter what is happening externally.

Today, close your eyes for a moment. Breathe. Feel the stillness beneath everything.

I create inner stillness,
allowing peace to arise from within.

Saying Yes to What Is

Life is not always what we expect, but resisting reality only creates suffering. Saying yes to 'what is' does not mean we have to like it—it simply means we stop fighting against it. Acceptance allows us to move forward with clarity and ease.

Today, practice saying yes to this moment, exactly as it is. Notice how acceptance softens resistance.

I say yes to life as it is,
knowing that peace comes through acceptance.

DECEMBER 25

Moving Beyond Self-Doubt

Self-doubt keeps us small. It whispers that we are not ready, not enough, not capable. But self-doubt is just a story—not a truth. When we recognize it as such, we stop letting it control us and start stepping into our true potential.

Today, challenge a moment of self-doubt. Instead of believing it, ask: What if I trusted myself instead?

I move beyond self-doubt, trusting in my
own humble strength, wisdom, and unconditional worth.

DECEMBER 26

The Gift of Deep Breathing

The breath is always available—a tool for calm, clarity, and presence. When we breathe deeply, we send a signal to the body that it is safe, grounding ourselves in the moment. Conscious breathing is one of the simplest yet most powerful forms of self-care.

Today, take a few deep breaths. Feel the inhale expand, the exhale release. Let your breath bring you home.

I embrace deep breathing as a gift,
using it to center myself in the present moment.

DECEMBER 27

Every Ending is a Beginning

Nothing truly ends—it only transforms. Every goodbye carries the seed of a new hello. Every closed door opens space for something unexpected. When we trust in this cycle, we release fear of endings and welcome the beauty of what's to come.

Today, reflect on an ending in your life. Instead of mourning, see if you can recognize the beginning it created.

I trust that every ending is also a beginning,
allowing life to unfold naturally.

DECEMBER 28

You Are Already Whole

We often search for something to complete us—believing that happiness lies in the next achievement, relationship, or milestone. But beneath all seeking, we are already whole. Nothing outside of us can make us more complete than we already are.

Today, let go of the idea that something is missing. Rest in the truth that you are already enough.

I embrace my wholeness,
knowing that nothing is missing from who I really am.

DECEMBER 29

Closing the Year with Gratitude

As the year comes to a seeming end, gratitude allows us to reflect with appreciation and ironic humor. Not everything went as planned and most of everything that happened was beyond our illusion of personal control. Some things were difficult, others joyful. But each experience brought something valuable, if we allow the wisdom to shine from within. Gratitude does not mean everything was easy—it means we recognize the lessons, growth, and beauty that came through all of life's experiences.

Today, take a moment to reflect on the year. What are you grateful for? What about right now? What are you grateful for? Look around. Are you grateful for "seeing," "hearing," "smelling?" Let us not forget to always acknowledge the most obvious blessings of life.

I close this year with infinite gratitude
that is always here, honoring everything.

DECEMBER 30

Embracing the New Year with Openness

A new year symbolizes a blank canvas—an opportunity to welcome the unknown with curiosity and trust. Instead of making rigid resolutions for a future that doesn't exist, what if we simply set the intention to remain open, now? To embrace life as it unfolds, moment by moment?

Today, set an intention, not for the new year, but for right now—not for control, but for presence. Not for trying to get what you want, but for trusting the great mystery. Not for avoiding feeling, but for providing kind and loving attention to those places in your experience seeking acceptance and healing.

I step into right here now with openness,
trusting in life's unfolding. I welcome and allow all feelings and
sensations of the body to be as they are. I welcome everything!

The Journey Continues

The end of the year is not the end of this apparent journey of healing, feeling, and awakening as the Earth, traveling at 67,000 miles per hour, completes another trip around the Sun. The symbolic end and celebration of one year ushers in new possibilities, another step in the never-ending unfolding of life in this Divine Cosmic Mystery in which we appear. Growth, awareness, and presence continue, moment by moment beyond our personal control. And, that's okay. There is no finish line, only the ongoing experience of being alive in human form. Let if flow. Trust the process of life.

Today, trust that wherever you are is exactly where you need to be in the cosmos. The journey continues, and you are ready because you ARE here. You are always here as Infinite Loving Awareness.

As the uninvolved witness, I embrace the journey, knowing that life is always unfolding in perfect timeless time—in perfect harmony, even if the mind doesn't understand. Underneath the mind's ongoing mental activity and noise, there is this knowingness:

That regardless of what is happening, changing, arising and passing away in conscious awareness...

I AM HERE.

I AM Unchanging Timeless Loving Reality...

...From Which All Experience Arises.

APPENDIX I

About CHA

Collective Healing Anonymous (CHA) emerges as a groundbreaking non-religious, yet highly spiritual process and support group that goes beyond the limitations of traditional 12-step programs. Offering a fresh perspective rooted in collective consciousness and deep introspection, CHA offers a transformative path toward Self-Discovery, Healing, and everlasting Inner Freedom. CHA further provides the absolute potential to fully recover from any and all obsessions, compulsions, addictions, dependencies, and identity matters, in THIS LIFE! In short, Collective Healing Anonymous is a Revolutionary and Empowering Possibility to heal, feel, and awaken, together! www.discovercha.org

The CHA Basics Book

The CHA Basics book, in simple and relatable terms, shares CHA's foundational purpose, basic structure, and essential ingredients for fully understanding and participating in the CHA Process and Community. This guide also shares compassionate wisdom and guidance toward healing and awakening, what to expect when attending meetings, and the importance of including Sacred Processes in your life, as well as providing specific and easy to follow tips to begin living the life you know in your heart is possible. Lastly, detailed instructions about how to start and conduct a CHA gathering in your area are available in the Tool Box Section of this book.

Moving forward, to allow Collective Healing Anonymous to best work for you, it may be helpful to understand that CHA is not a belief system, philosophy, and not a religious teaching; does not ascribe to any single doctrine, guru, or spiritual master. It is, however, a supportive non-religious spiritual process and support system focused on collective healing through inner transformation and personal growth, using a variety of resources, even science; and focusing on CHA's official 12 steps to liberation.

Another highly relevant consideration is this: CHA can be used as a companion to any 12-step or non-12-step program, healing and awakening modality like yoga, or counseling process you may be utilizing. Unlike programs that demand exclusivity, CHA embraces absolute inclusivity, recognizing that healing and growth can come from a variety of sources. This flexibility allows individuals to integrate the CHA process with their existing practices without conflict, enhancing their overall journey; which easily supports and complements other methods by offering an additional layer of depth and understanding. By not mandating exclusivity, and also providing the option to establish your own steps, CHA empowers individuals to create a personalized and holistic trajectory to their healing and awakening. This approach naturally nurtures a more comprehensive and fulfilling path to self-discovery, while connecting with a community of like-minded friends steeped in collective wisdom. Other available resources, references and literature may be found at the CHA's official website: www.DiscoverCHA.org.

APPENDIX II

Foundational Themes of CHA

It's Okay

This reassures you that whatever you're feeling or going through is acceptable and neither makes you a good nor bad person. "It's okay" is an acknowledgment that everyone faces challenges, and it's perfectly natural to seek out help and humbly receive support, unconditionally.

You are not Alone

This reminds you there are others who have experienced similar struggles, and somehow opens the door to dissolving the idea of disconnection holding us back from coming out of our shell and truly blossoming.

We are Here for You

This underscores the healing power of a support system. It means that there are people who will not judge or condemn you, who genuinely care about your well-being, and are unconditionally willing to assist you on your journey. You do not have to face your struggles in isolation.

There is Another Way to Be Alive

This offers inspirational and life-liberating energy and possibility there are alternative paths to living a fulfilling and meaningful life beyond our habits, routines, and beliefs no longer serving us. It encourages you to explore new possibilities and creativity beyond your current struggles.

You Have Choices

This empowers you by reminding us that we have the agency and power to make decisions about our lives. You wield the power of choice to consciously choose healthier and more constructive paths; recognizing you are NOT bound by your past choices, beliefs, feelings, and behaviors.

You Are Allowed

This is about giving ourselves permission to think, feel, and express ourselves beyond our critical inner voices. We are allowed to have the experience we are having right here now, without trying to mentally change it or judge it. You are allowed to be exactly as you already are. Perfectly whole.

You are Already Whole, Worthy, Innocent, Complete, Enough

This highlights your everlasting, natural, and intrinsic innocence, worthiness and completeness. It signifies that you do not need external validation or to modify your behavior or use substances to feel whole. You are already complete, lovable, enough, just as you are; always! Even when acting out addictions.

APPENDIX III

The 12 Steps of Collective Healing Anonymous

1. We humbly acknowledge the impact of [the coping mechanism dependency] on our lives, understanding it is only temporary, and embrace the powers within us to reclaim autonomy of our minds.

2. We opened to the possibility that the power to restore conscious clarity resides within ourselves, and that we can utilize this Universal Loving Force and inner strength as Trust, Compassion, Gratitude, Diligent Focus, and Willingness, while utilizing relevant external guidance and support whenever we so choose.

3. Made a conscious decision to turn to and trust the deeper and silent wisdom and Universal Loving Intelligence within, choosing to rely on this inner guidance rather than being driven solely by our conditioning, mental will, thoughts, obsessions, and compulsions. By embracing this inner wisdom, our false identities gradually dissolve as awareness of our essential, already whole, inseparable being emerges.

4. By acknowledging our primal innocence, we made a compassionate and fearlessly honest inventory of self judgments we have been carrying in the mind.

5. Admitted to our Universal Self, our personal self, and to another human being the exact nature of our believed self judgments. (Hint: All three are one in the same.)

6. Were entirely ready to free ourselves from ALL self criticism, self judgment, self blame, guilt, and unworthiness by allowing ourselves to feel whatever we have been avoiding.

7. Humbly sought inwardly through meditative self-inquiry

to compassionately observe and understand the innocent nature of our beliefs, behaviors, feelings, and suffering.

8. Made a list of all persons we believe we have harmed and became willing to make amends to them all.

9. Made direct amends to such people wherever possible, except when to do so would injure them, others, or myself.

10. Continued to remain mindful and alert to unnecessary inner dialogue and judgmental thoughts, as well as externalized speech and behaviors; and when we believed we caused harm, promptly admitted it.

11. Sought through meditation, self-inquiry, and various other Sacred Processes to fully understand and become aware of the nature of suffering, experience, divine reality, and mySELF; thereby completely dissolving the illusion of separation and unwholeness.

12. Having become deeply healed and awakened through the power of awareness, we continue allowing life to effortlessly flow with ease, balance, and grace, while our lives effortlessly unfold beyond personal identity and both the illusion of control and separation.

APPENDIX IV

The Essence of the Peace President Collection of Books

A Collection of Books as Guidance toward Inner Transformation, Conscious Government, and Peaceful Coexistence

[Please note that this book, "Rejoice Now - 365 Days of Loving Inspiration and Reflection" is NOT part of the Peace President Collection.

For decades to centuries to millennia past, human beings have been struggling with one another, fighting, blaming—arguing over who is right or wrong, good or bad. Governments and civilizations continue rising and falling while unnecessary social divides and war persist. Regardless of the era, whether played out in ancient to medieval times or modern day, conflict appears to be arising from one set of beliefs and identities versus another set of beliefs and identities; as if there are two or more sets of rigid opinions in opposition to each other, always.

Could it be that we are often unaware of solutions to our challenges because we were born into cultures defined by divisive identities and conflicting traditions—cultures that treat these self-generated divisions as socially acceptable? We may simply not know any better, and relying solely on the limited perceptions we have been taught to trust. Perhaps we have yet to question the true validity of those beliefs and assumptions. For instance, why are there two political parties always divided instead of one unified party that is all inclusive? One nation, undivided? A genuinely United States?

An Intimate and Personal Story

I recall feeling so deeply depressed, constrained, and frozen, as if living life was more like being caught in an amusement park of suffering, where I was living the same day over and over—like the movie 'Groundhog's Day'—lost in a day of tension, stress, anxiety—always in search of finding pleasant sensations while avoiding unpleasant feelings. Apparently, I thought, and believed, I was happy, yet discovered 'my' happiness was conditional—greatly limited—limiting the reality of unconditional joyous peace always present underneath whatever appears to be happening. Little did I know this was happening: I was becoming accustomed to avoiding feeling while a type of numbness was accumulating; specifically due to living in a socially accepted survival mode of self-preservation deemed 'normal' by practically everyone! In other words, I was unconsciously lost trying and striving to become someone or something I was not, trying to appease others, and fit into a world and society which seemed to be going in the wrong direction.

You see, I was born into a beautifully creative, loving, and wonderful world, yet highly destructive. A world of human consciousness where war, violence, greed, and learning to deny my experience and intuition was the cultural norm; which is to say: For most of my life, I was unaware that my self-defeating programming and conditioning being acted out as unconscious reactions and self-defeating compulsions were dictating my life. I was completely unaware or in denial of this: that I had been manipulating my mind to adapt to a profoundly sick society, because that is what everyone said to do! Basically, I was going with the crowd of self-destructive cultural patterns that were socially acceptable, instead of questioning the legitimacy of them. In other words, it seemed easier, somehow, to live in denial, than confront what was really happening; even though the cultural, personal, and family patterns I had been relying on to provide a sense of security, self worth, and happiness, were deeply unsettling, and only temporarily fulfilling at best.

The Profound Possibility

Of course, the society or world, as human collective consciousness in which I was born, wields absolute potential to transcend any and ALL self-defeating personal, societal, national, global, and generational thought habits, behavioral patterns, and mind-made divisions. Yet, that insight or realization did not arise until much later in life, when somehow, I became aware of this: that what I had been trained and taught to believe would bring everlasting fulfillment, peace, joy, and prosperity, was never going to work. (The keyword there is everlasting.) So, obviously, there was great confusion, self-judgment and hatred that developed, and ongoing apathy for the world, and learned self-oppression resulting from trying to fit into social patterns and concepts that simply "don't work." A big part of the belief system of self-contempt that developed was due to this: believing I was a failure or not good enough because the happiness promised by trusting what I had been conditioned to believe would bring everlasting feelings of worthiness and wholeness never proved to be true. So, of course, no matter how hard I attempted to 'follow the rules' and advice programmed and conditioned into my mind over the years, it never brought forth what was promised; no matter what I did, said, thought, believed, or identified with. What a wildly amazing moment of conscious clarity—to acknowledge the possibility that virtually everything I was told about living a life of happiness, joy, peace, and prosperity—was utterly untrue, in reality.

However, despite the tremendous inner turmoil building throughout my life and denying sacred wisdom deep within my being, I somehow always knew in my heart that a life free of suffering, unworthiness, division, violence, and fear, was possible; a truer life not only in and as myself, but a truer possibility for Humanity as a whole. At the time, I had not yet become aware there is a choice, a profoundly conscious choice each and every one of us can acknowledge: To choose self-destructive patterns, victimhood, and denial—OR—productive life liberating sacred processes and sacred human qualities toward inner wellbeing, unimaginable joy, and profound conscious clarity.

Through what I refer to as Sacred Processes of Awakening like meditation, this awareness illuminated itself: Every human being on the planet is capable of waking up to the truth of us—our most compassionate and loving and generous nature, absent of the illusion of separation, and free of our innocently self-destructive tendencies.

We need only willingly open, somehow, to those possibilities amid our resistance and compulsions to avoid what we know in our hearts to be true. Perhaps, by embracing the healing and life liberating powers of humility and forgiveness. Somehow when one wholeheartedly becomes interested in the most sacred qualities like humility and forgiveness and patience, we begin acknowledging there is another way to live. We also begin opening to possibilities beyond our wildest dreams, like this: that we can free ourselves from self-judgment permanently, heal unattended sorrow forever, and come out of hiding, whenever we so choose.

Could it be we continue venturing down our generational paths of suffering as anxiety, ill content, blame, worry, stress, and division, because we are adverse to possibilities that may require radical self-honesty and inner transformation? Could our self sustained power struggles, misery, greed, and violence be asking for conscious clarity and peaceful and compassionate understanding, versus the unhelpful mental strategy of accusing, criticizing, blaming, and judging ourselves that sustain the confusion, despair, unworthiness, divisions, conflict, and rigid viewpoints—both individually and collectively? Let us not fret. There is a choice in the matter. There is Good News! This is another way to be, alive!

Opening unto Feeling, Healing, Awakening

By inspiring us to partake in Sacred Processes toward inner liberation, conscious government, and peaceful coexistence, the essence of the Peace President Collection of Books and Peace President United is this: To invite and embrace healing, feeling, and awakening unto the loving truth of us, by willingly opening to new possibilities for ourselves, our nation, government, and humanity as a whole, beyond our socially acceptable divisive beliefs and identities, painful habits, and self-destructive trends.

Practically speaking: Although, as Humanity, as citizens of countries and respective governments, who harness the most amazing potential and life liberating qualities capable of enhancing wellbeing, and providing vital necessities and basic human needs to everyone on earth, we appear to be innocently asleep, suffering, confused, unconscious, and mostly unaware of our individual and collective self-destructive, neglectful, and divisive momentum; as well as our most loving and greatest possibilities! In other words, we are unaware of our absolutely amazing and loving all inclusive potential, because our attention seems to be focused elsewhere!

We appear to be innocently lost in the grip of judgment and greed, and blaming anyone and ourselves while rationalizing and justifying those divisive and hurtful energies—regardless if those thoughts and actions are destructive and sustain unnecessary turmoil, violence, unworthiness, and separation. Remember, there is Good News! There exists the absolute possibility to Coexist Peacefully beyond blame, hatred, suffering, division, and destruction; that is, when we open our hearts and minds to new possibilities, the truth of ourselves, and Universal Vision.

Perhaps, amid our resistance to genuinely and willingly acknowledging our greatest all inclusive and loving potential, we must first welcome self-forgiveness and the infinite grace of gratitude, mercy, and abundance.

There is Good News! Are you open to the possibilities? Have we finally had enough of the old ideas and habits leading us down a path of destruction, disconnection, division, confusion, despair, and violence? Have we had enough of denying ourselves our most loving and all inclusive sacred qualities such as compassion and humility? Isn't it time for foundational changes and transformation in our individual lives and as a nation to unfold in the most loving and unifying manner; even if those essential shifts may be uncomfortable and unsettling for a little while?

The "Peace President Collection" of books offers awareness and poignant suggestions, guidance, and solutions to our individual yearning for inner peace and collective calling for positive change beyond division and conflict. These works acknowledge the urgency of embracing new possibilities and transcending old patterns that have led us astray—patterns of division, confusion, blame, and violence. Through Sacred Processes and by embracing our most Sacred Human Qualities, like compassion and humility, this wisdom is calling for foundational changes and transformation, both individually and as a nation; and world.

The Peace President Collection reminds us that while such shifts may be uncomfortable initially, they hold the promise of a more loving, unified, and peaceful future, not only for ourselves, but most importantly, for future generations. It is an invitation to seize the opportunity for lasting change and to consciously choose the path of feeling, healing, and awakening.

With Timeless Love,

Peace President

www.peacepresidentunited.org

www.ingramcontent.com/pod-product-compliance
Lightning Source LLC
Chambersburg PA
CBHW021903020426
42334CB00013B/452